INTERNATIONAL THEATRE AND CINEMA

EDITED BY HERBERT MARSHALL

CIVIC THEATRE DESIGN

RICHARD LEACROFT

A.R.I.B.A. A.A.HONS. DIPL.

Civic Theatre Design

WITH ILLUSTRATIONS BY THE AUTHOR

London

DENNIS DOBSON LTD

First published in Great Britain in MCMXLIX by DENNIS DOBSON
LTD, 12 Park Place, St James's, London SW1. All rights reserved.
Printed in Great Britain by THE BOWERING PRESS, Plymouth.
145/R

© 1949

Contents

Illustrations

Acknowledgments

I wish to express my gratitude to all who have helped me in different ways in the preparation of this book: in particular MR A. B. LACY, A.R.I.B.A. and MR J. E. WHEELER for their various architectural suggestions and MR OSBORNE ROBINSON for permission to quote freely from his twenty-one years' experience as designer to the Northampton Repertory Theatre. Finally I owe a particular debt of gratitude to my wife, and to MR S. H. REED for valuable help in the preparation of the text and in the reading of proofs.

1. *Introduction*

IT CAN SAFELY be said that, hitherto, theatre workers have given but little constructive thought to specifying their maximum and minimum requirements for the guidance of the theatre architect; indeed, it would appear that the back-stage regions in particular have usually been kept a profound secret. This makes life very difficult for the architect commissioned to design a new theatre, for even though he be a theatre-goer, he will rarely know, for example, how scenery is built up or how it is used, moved, and stored. Added to this he will know little or nothing of the many specialized appliances in common use, or the names and technical terms which, to his constant mystification, fall so lightly from the theatre technician's lips in the course of professional discussion.[1]

The architect who does not possess a reasonable background knowledge, both of theatre history and modern practice, is bound to be at a loss when making decisions in matters of design; especially as theatre technicians are by no means always in agreement among themselves, being influenced to some extent by the type of theatre in which they are accustomed to work, and tending to be impatient of any suggestion of a different form of theatre.

In this book an attempt has been made to present, very briefly, an introduction to the subject of theatre design which it is hoped will provide the sponsors and architects of our future civic theatres with valuable background knowledge, and, at the same time, to set before them some working suggestions on the design of this type of theatre. These

[1] See; *Glossary of Technical Theatrical Terms*, Strand Electric, 1947, 2*s*. *A Short Glossary of Theatrical Terms* by W. G. Fay, French's. *Stage Management* by Peter Bax, Lovatt Dickson, 1936. See also: an illustrated glossary in *The Essentials of Stage Planning*.

suggestions are the result of personal observation made possible by a good many years of work in scenic design in the varied conditions provided by the repertory theatre up and down the country; since such theatres will form the nucleus of the future civic theatres they provide excellent material for the purpose of this study. It would be of great value if similar personal reports by other theatre workers, actors, directors, producers, electricians, and stage staff could be compiled as contributions towards presenting the theatre architect with as many aspects of the problem as it is possible to provide.

The literature of theatre design is scanty, and, unfortunately, it is not only the present-day theatre that suffers in this way. Little enough is known of the history of British theatre architecture in general, and, although much research is being carried out on the theatres of the last few centuries, few results have as yet been published.[2]

The theatres of the eighteenth and nineteenth centuries warrant careful study by the modern theatre designer. From them he will learn much of the relationship traditionally existing between the British audience and the actor; and will acquire a perspective which will enable him to understand the present tendency towards a return to the earlier intimacy which existed between them.

[2] *Theatre Royal, Bristol* by John Summerson, Architectural Review, December 1943. *The Stage Groove and Thunder Run* by Richard Southern, Architectural Review, May 1944. *The Georgian Theatre at Richmond* by Richard Southern, Architectural Review, January 1945. *Interesting Matter related to the Theatre Royal, at Ipswich,* Architectural Review, August 1946. *The Georgian Playhouse* by Richard Southern, Pleiades Books Ltd., 1948. *Theatre Notebook.* A Quarterly of Notes and Research, including *The Bulletin of the Society for Theatre Research.*

2. *Historical Survey*

Drama originally developed from the pagan religious festivals which made use of a dramatic ritual and a particular form of setting or building for their services and sacrifices. Stonehenge, for example, provided the necessary setting for the enacting of a particular drama of ritual sacrifice, and it is interesting to note that it embodies in its shape the fundamental plan which is a characteristic of the classic theatre design—the circle.

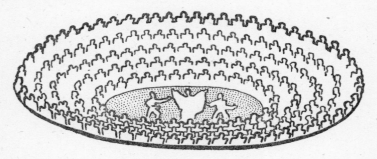

Fig. 1. Primary theatre form

From the simple religious origin developed a definite drama requiring a special theatre for its performance. This development is first observable outside Britain: the first signs of organized drama in this country are those brought by the Romans, and their coming brings the first glimmer of light into the history of our subject.

The development towards a definite theatre building began when it was realized that only the front few rows of the audience could see and hear the actor properly, and those seated behind raised themselves in some convenient manner so as to see over the heads of those seated in front (see Fig. 1). Where there was a natural bowl in the country-side it was chosen as an ideal spot for outdoor performances, as here

the audience could sit one above the other on the slopes of
the bowl. For dance or ritual the audience seated all around
the area made an ideal arrangement, but when the drama
proper began to develop, the need for the story-teller and
his assistants to address themselves to the audience, caused
the latter to arrange themselves around two-thirds of a circle
facing the actor, whilst the area directly behind him was left
empty. A valley in the hillside became the chosen ground
then, and the audience looked down towards the actor while
the country-side stretched out behind him, a natural and

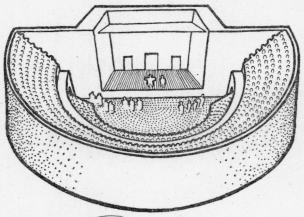

Fig. 2. Classic theatre form

beautiful setting which, in later ages, came to be replaced by
the scenery with which modern audiences are familiar. This
hillside was soon built up with wooden seats for greater comfort; later these in turn were replaced by stone. The actor
was raised on a platform so that he could be seen and heard
more easily, while the 'chorus' stayed on the flat ground at
his feet.

As the drama developed into a popular art people sought
to be entertained in places where there were no hillsides, and
so an artificial hill had to be created and 'theatres' were built
which had great semi-circular banks of seating supported on
stone vaults enclosed by a great wall. Facing the seating was

a raised rectangular stage, with a semi-circular choral area in front, backed by a great wall behind which were the changing rooms for the actors (see Fig. 2). An archway, known as a 'parados', led into either side of the choral area, and there were three doorways in the wall at the rear of the stage. The whole building was a reproduction in stone of the theatre characteristics of the original hillside, with the 'skene' or rear wall replacing the natural setting. From this developed the form of theatre which the Romans built in Britain for the performance of their own dramas, and the remains of such a theatre can still be seen at St Albans.

The Britons themselves had not yet developed any definite form of drama, and when the Romans were evacuated it was left to the Minstrels and story-tellers to continue the history. We can still see remains today of their early efforts in drama in the mummers and other remnants of pagan festivals, e.g. the Minehead Hobby Horse, and the mummers of Andover and Marshfield. As yet, however, there were no special theatre buildings, and such performances as there were, were simply given in the halls of the great houses.

It is not until the tenth century that we find the first sign of organized drama in this country, when the clergy began to dramatize the chief religious festivals for the benefit of an illiterate populace. The 'plays' told in dramatic form, the various stories from the life of Christ, but it was soon found that the churches, where they were first performed, were not large enough to accommodate both congregation and performers, and the action of the play therefore moved outside the church into the churchyard. As these plays became more and more popular the clergy became nervous as to the results of their action and did their best to check any further development; but already the newly-born theatre was a lusty infant, and it rapidly passed out of the hands of the clergy into those of the town guilds.

When the plays were performed inside the church, the actors moved from one point in the church to another as the story developed: fixed places represented the manger,

Herod's court, the tomb, etc., and when the plays were taken
outside the church this arrangement still persisted. By the
fifteenth century, however, when the town guilds were organ-
izing the plays, each section of the play was performed on
a different 'pageant' or wagon. Each guild was given a portion of the religious story to portray, and provided the actors
and equipment. Service was voluntary, and on the public
feast days the people came to watch, and take part in, the
performances. Each guild had its own pageant consisting of
an upper and lower room; in the lower, curtained, room the

Fig. 3. Medieval theatre form

players dressed and prepared for the play, and on the upper
and in the surrounding street they performed. Each pageant
in turn took up its position at previously assigned vantage
points in the town.

The general architectural aspect of this new form of drama
adhered very closely to the primary theatrical arrangement:
the actors appeared on a raised platform set in the centre of
an open space, entirely surrounded by their audience, and, a
point firmly to be borne in mind throughout the rest of this
book, in direct contact with their audience (see Fig. 3).

It soon became necessary to provide drama at times other

than feast days, and as the patronage of the guilds was with-drawn there grew up companies of strolling players who gave their plays in any convenient buildings. Usually the per-formances took place in the inn-yards of the towns which they visited. The inns were mostly similar in shape and plan: the buildings were grouped around a rectangular yard, the various rooms being accessible from open galleries overlook-ing the yard, and approached by stairs at each corner. To these buildings came the strolling players with their proper-ties and costumes in their cart. Entering through an archway leading from the street, they set the cart or platform at the far end of the yard against a wall where they had easy access to one of the inn rooms which they used as a dressing-room. In cases where an upper room or balcony was needed for the action of the play, the inn gallery directly above their platform would be brought into use. The majority of the audience stood in the yard, while the residents of the inn and privileged persons looked down on the performance from the surrounding galleries: still the actor was in direct contact with his audience.

When in 1576, James Burbage built the first British play-house, known as the 'Theatre', for his company of strolling players, he probably based his design partly on the inn-yards in which his company was accustomed to play, and partly on the classic theatre (compare Figs. 2 and 4). Other theatres followed, and, except for the Fortune which was rectangular in plan, were mostly of a shape conforming to a rough circle. As far as we know the buildings were not over-large, and their general arrangement was very probably on the follow-ing lines: around a central yard or 'pit' were grouped two or three galleries, arranged one above the other with seats for the spectators, very like the galleries around the inn-yards. Projecting into the yard at ground level, and occupying about half its area, was a raised stage which was partly covered by a roof. Above the roof was a small room where machinery could be worked to enable gods to ascend from, and descend to, the stage, and there was at least one trap in the stage floor to enable persons to ascend from below, and for use as a grave. At the rear of the stage was an 'inner room' which was open to the stage proper, but could be curtained off from it; on either side of this was a door leading to the dressing-rooms, these doors formed the main entrances to the stage. The dressing-rooms were arranged on either side of the inner room, and on either side of these were the rooms for the

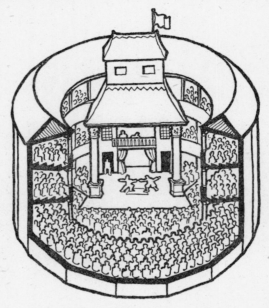

Fig. 4. Elizabethan theatre form

gentlemen of the audience who either sat here and viewed the stage, or later sat on the stage itself and used the rooms as retiring rooms. Over the stage was a gallery, and flanking this on either side were windows placed over the entrance doors to the stage; all of these could be used by the actors when so required by the action of the play. The arrangement of the inner room and side doors parallelled very closely the arrangements of the doors in the 'skene' of the classic theatre.[1]

[1] *Introducing Shakespeare* by G. B. Harrison, Pelican Book A 43, Penguin Books, 1939. *Shakespeare and the Players* by C. Walter Hodges, Ernest Benn

Here then are assembled together in one building most of the features which have persisted in theatre buildings down to the present day. Two features, however, are lacking: in the first place these Elizabethan theatres were open to the sky, and audience and actor alike were lit by daylight, the plays being performed in the afternoons; the other feature, found as yet in very small quantities, is scenery, and it is the gradual development of this in the theatre which accounts for the majority of changes that later took place in theatre design.

It was not long, however, before it was realized that an indoor theatre would have many advantages over these open air theatres: it could for example be used in any weather. Already many private theatres were in use at Court and in private houses, stages and seating being built-up in a large hall to designs based on the theatres of Italy, which, in turn, were based on the Renaissance idea of the classical Roman theatre. These theatres made prominent use of a painted 'proscenium arch' which separated the new 'painted scenery' from the audience.

In 1642 the Puritans closed all the theatres and, until the Restoration in 1660, the drama was driven underground; when it reappeared, it was in new theatres which based their designs on the earlier private theatres. These new buildings included features from both the earlier forms of theatre, but in place of the circular plan the new designs were for rectangular buildings, these being a more convenient shape for roofing. The new theatres were still very small (see Fig. 5), but the large stage of the Elizabethan type was incorporated in the new form; the open pit was now filled in with benches, and its floor was sloped-up away from the stage to provide better sight lines, both stage and pit being now roughly rectangular in plan. On either side of the stage and pit were two

Ltd., 1948. *Shakespeare Survey*, an annual survey of Shakespearian study and production, edited by Allardyce Nicoll, Cambridge University Press, 1948. *The Elizabethan Theatre* by Sir E. K. Chalmers, 4 vols., Oxford Press, 1923.

tiers of boxes, and at the rear of the pit, opposite to the stage, were open galleries. The two doors with windows over, which were set at the rear of the earlier stage, are now moved to the side walls of the 'auditorium', and give entrance to either side of the stage. In many cases the function of the upper gallery and windows of the earlier form were combined by arranging a box or small gallery over each entrance door.

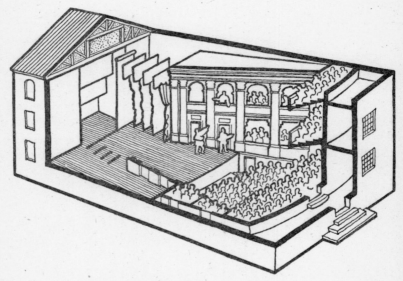

Fig. 5. Restoration theatre form

The main advance in design which these buildings incorporated was the addition of a large stage area at the rear of the 'fore-stage', replacing the earlier inner stage with balcony over, for use with the extremely complicated scenery which now became the fashion. The scenic effects were cut off from the audience by the proscenium arch; this, however, was no elaborate construction such as we know today, but was simply the point at which the side walls (forming the front of the boxes) and the ceiling of the auditorium ended, and the stage widened out to the full width and height of the building to provide accommodation for the machinery which was needed to work the scenic effects. At the centre back of the rear-stage there was an extra depth of stage for use with deep vistas of scenery, and on either side and above this were the dressing-rooms. The fore-stage and rear-stage sloped up, away from the audience, to increase the effect of perspective which was aimed at in the design of the scenery. In some cases the design of the auditorium itself was carried out in perspective to help in achieving unity of design. This feature may well have had an excellent effect in concentrating the attention of the audience on the stage; it also helped to increase the feeling of intimacy which was already created by the small size of the theatre, and by the arrangement of the audience around the actor, who still performed mainly on the fore-stage, the rear-stage being reserved for scenic effects. In place of daylight the entire theatre was lit by candlelight, and it was now possible to arrange special lighting effects amidst the scenery; the lights of the auditorium, however, were left burning during the whole performance.

The basic plan for the traditional British theatre had now been reached, and the theatre still retained the intimacy which was apparent in the pageant, in the inn, and in the Elizabethan playhouse.

During the seventeenth century the theatres, which until now had been run on a co-operative basis by the whole company, came under the control of commercial managements, and it was their desire for large profits which caused the gradual deterioration of theatre design. Their first move was to cut back the fore-stage, thereby extending the pit. The proscenium or stage doors, which until now had been used for all entrances to and exits from the stage, were replaced by boxes for the audience, thus causing the actor to make his entrance on to the stage from amidst the scenery. This movement continued until the end of the nineteenth century when the last vestige of fore-stage and proscenium door disappeared. While the actor was being pushed further and further away from the audience, until he was finally shut off from them behind the present day proscenium opening (see Fig. 6), the old intimacy between actor and audience was further strained to breaking point by the fact that the commercially minded owners built larger and larger theatres, which placed a great part of the audience beyond easy vocal reach of the actor. When, in 1830, gas light replaced candle-light, the picture-frame effect was heightened by the fact that the lights in the auditorium could now be turned down

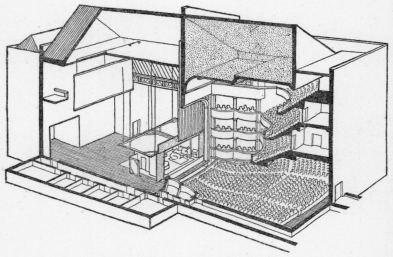

Fig. 6. Contemporary picture-frame form

during the performance, and the stage lighting be controlled to give varied effects. The use of naked lights in the theatre naturally constituted a great fire risk, especially as the major part of the stage equipment was of timber and the scenery of canvas, and it is from this date that the restrictions which so bind theatre design today are dated. The later replacement of gas by electricity did much to remedy this defect, but the damage was already done.

During the early years of the nineteenth century the pit, which till now had been enclosed by the first tier of boxes, was extended to fill the full width of the auditorium, and the tiers of boxes were raised to give headroom under. These boxes were gradually removed to give more seating in the form of open galleries or circles. The rectangular shape of the auditorium had, very early in this process, been rounded off until it reached a horse-shoe shape, and this shape persisted in spite of the fact that it created very bad sight-lines from a large number of the seats to the now totally enclosed stage.

What of the stage during this period? Apart from the fact that the fore-stage had been gradually removed, very little change had taken place. The stage of our contemporary theatres is much like those of the seventeenth and eighteenth centuries in plan, it is only the section and the equipment

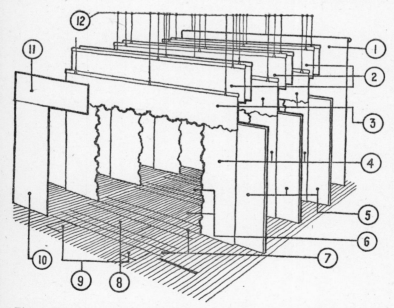

Fig. 7. Diagram illustrating the wing and border setting, and the parts of the traditional stage

1, backcloth on roller. 2, additional borders for further settings. 3, borders for setting in use on stage. 4, wings for setting in use on stage. 5, additional wings for further settings. 6, bridges. 7, sliders. 8, grave trap. 9, corner traps. 10, permanent wing or tormentor. 11, permanent border or teaser. 12, lines from grid.

which vary. What was this equipment, and how much of it, if any, is of use in the modern theatre? The final development (see Fig. 7), which persisted until the latter part of the nineteenth century was to dispose the scenery upon the stage in the form of a number of painted wings, set one behind the other, parallel with the front of the stage; with these wings were arranged shutters which could form a complete backing to a scene and, when no longer required, could slide apart to reveal a further scene. All these pieces were moved in grooves arranged in groups of three or four, thus allowing for the provision of three or four different sets of scenery, each set representing a different stock scene. The grooves were arranged at either side of the stage and were fastened to the floor, and corresponding sets of grooves, to take the tops of the wings and shutters, were fastened to the floor of the 'fly-galleries' which were built above, and on either side of, the stage. These galleries were used for the disposal of the equipment which regulated the movement of scenery hung above the stage. This scenery took the form of a series of borders, or lengths of cloth fixed to battens, which spanned the stage from one side to the other, and were hung in sets to match the side wings. Backcloths were also used, but these had to be wound up on rollers when no longer required, as it was not until the last quarter of the nineteenth century that the roof over the stage was raised high enough to enable backcloths to be raised up out of sight or 'flown'.

To enable this new movement to be performed the theatre was equipped with a grid or open floor placed high above the stage, and on this floor pulleys were arranged in sets spaced at from 12 in. to 18 in. centres from front to back of the stage (see Fig. 8). Each set consisted of three pulleys and a headblock; one pulley was placed directly above the centre of the stage, and the two further pulleys were arranged from 12 ft. to 15 ft. on either side of this centre pulley. A headblock was also fixed on the grid approximately 6 ft. from the side wall of the theatre, usually the left-hand side as you stand on the stage facing the audience. Three lines, a 'long', 'centre', and 'short', each reaching to stage level, were led over their respective pulleys and carried to the headblock where all the ropes descended to the fly-gallery and were tied off around a cleat fixed to the gallery rail.

In order to raise a backcloth into the air, the stage ends of the lines were made fast to the top batten of the cloth, and, when all was ready, men situated on the fly-gallery hauled on all three lines at the same time until the cloth was hanging

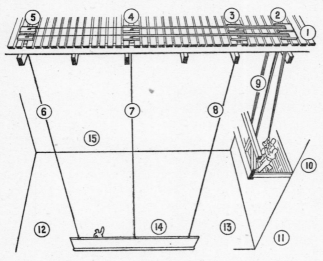

Fig. 8. Diagram illustrating the traditional flying system

1, grid. 2, headblock. 3, short pulley. 4, centre pulley. 5, long pulley. 6, long line. 7, centre line. 8, short line. 9, lines tied to cleats on fly-rail. 10, fly-gallery. 11, stage level. 12, O.P. wing. 13, prompt wing. 14, backcloth tied off to a set of lines. 15, rear wall of stage.

with its bottom batten touching the stage, when the cloth was no longer required it was hauled higher up until it touched the under-side of the grid.

In addition to this vertical movement of scenery above the stage, provision was made in the stage floor whereby the central portions of the stage could be drawn off to either side, leaving a series of openings the full width of the proscenium opening in length, which were arranged in varying widths (see Fig. 7). Through the narrow openings thus provided,

'groundrows', that is, horizontal pieces of scenery representing landscapes, rocks, etc., could be raised from the basement
below, while the wider openings allowed for the raising of
large bridges on which whole groups of performers could
appear, as if by magic, from the depths beneath. In addition
to these a number of smaller openings were provided in the
form of traps, one small corner trap on either side of the stage
near the front, and further back in the centre a larger 'grave
trap', which was used on such occasions as a performance of
the graveyard scene in *Hamlet*. In addition to the appearances
from below, gods and goddesses could descend from the
heavens above, and for this purpose narrow bridges were
arranged at differing heights above the stage linking the two
fly-galleries together, these bridges were also used for the
adjustment of hanging scenery. The rear wall of the stage
was usually apportioned to the use of the scenic artist, and a
gallery or room at the level of the fly-gallery was used as a
paint-room. A large paint-frame, to which the scenery could
be fixed, was placed so that it could be wound up and down
past the paint-room floor thus enabling the painter to reach
any part of the scenery which he wished to paint.

Although there was a front curtain, it was not used after
the commencement of the play, and all the various scene
changes took place in full view of the audience.[2]

With the introduction of a more naturalistic style of play
in the latter half of the nineteenth century, the style of
scenery changed. The wings set parallel with the footlights,
and painted in perspective were replaced by scenery set to
follow the walls of a room, and painted to look as like a real
room as it was possible to achieve with paint and canvas. Thus
the 'box-set', or room with its fourth wall missing, was born

[2] See: An article on *The Stage Machinery of the Theatre Royal, Leicester*,
by Richard Southern and Richard Leacroft, in Wood, August 1948. *The
Development of the Theatre* by Allardyce Nicoll, Harrap, 1937. *Stuart Masques
and the Renaissance Stage* by Allardyce Nicoll, Harrap, 1937. *The Restoration
Theatre* by Montague Summers, Kegan Paul, 1937. *The History of the English
Theatre*, in six parts, by Richard Southern, Common Ground Film strips,
CGB 1, 2, 3 and 4.

(see Fig. 9). As soon as the scenery was set to follow the natural lines of the room it cut across the traps, bridges, and other openings in the stage floor, rendering their use no longer a feasible proposition, with the result that the use of these and of the grooves, died a natural death. The now old-fashioned form of wing and border setting still persists in some theatres for outdoor scenes, but its use has been largely outmoded by the introduction of the cyclorama, or large sky-cloth.

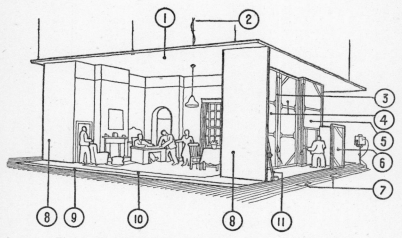

Fig. 9. Diagram illustrating the contemporary box setting

1, ceiling. 2, line and electric cable to hanging lamp. 3, cleat line joining flats together. 4, plain flats. 5, door flat. 6, door backing. 7, electric dips or traps. 8, tormentors. 9, carpet cut. 10, stage cloth. 11, extending brace and weight.

When the system of stage floor openings became obsolete they were replaced, in some cases, by stages built with sections which could rise or fall by hydraulic or, later, electric power, thereby providing a large variety of stage and acting levels. A current example can be seen installed at the Shakespeare Memorial Theatre at Stratford-on-Avon.[3]

The traditional theatre, in its later stages, demanded a definite architectural shape, which it would be well to note,

[3] *Modern Opera Houses and Theatres* by E. O. Sachs and E. A. Woodward, 1896–9.

as it has not yet been superseded by any later form: a high stage allowing space for backcloths to be hung and stored over the acting area, wide wing spaces, each the width of half the proscenium opening, to enable the sections of the stage floor to be drawn off to either side, a fly-gallery above the stage on either side, and a deep basement below the stage into which the bridges and scenery could sink. Until built-up naturalistic scenery replaced the few stock sets of scenes painted in perspective on flat wings, little space for the storage of scenery was required, as these stock scenes were used for any and every play; but, as naturalistic scenery was heavy and cumbersome, a storage space, or scene dock, had to be provided, where complete pieces of built-scenery could be stored. Scenery in the majority of present-day theatres is built and painted specially for each play, usually by an outside specialist firm, and therefore space for building and painting scenery has not been a requirement of the modern London theatre. It is here that the civic theatre differs widely from the current run of modern theatres, in that it requires to build, prepare and store on its own premises the scenery for a large number of productions; because of this fact it requires unique back-stage treatment.

From this brief survey it will probably be clear that all is not well with the contemporary treatment of theatre design, since it is so strongly influenced by the developments which took place during the nineteenth century, and, indeed, many of the theatres in use today, especially in the provinces, date from this period. The requirements of the new civic theatre must be considered in some detail to see what suggestions can be made to overcome these difficulties.

3. General Approach

PRESENT-DAY NEEDS IN theatre design can be divided into five categories, each type presenting its own particular problem. Briefly the list is as follows:

A. The Experimental theatre—1. University theatre.
                                        2. Drama school theatre.[1]
B. The National theatre.
C. The Civic theatre.
D. The Commercial theatre.
E. The Civic assembly hall and the School or Village hall.

Types A and B will be limited in numbers, and the majority of the theatres of the future are likely to fall into classes C, D and E. Types A, B and E, however, demand special consideration because of their individual needs, and do not come within the scope of this book. It is chiefly type C which is dealt with here, but many of the points which suit this type of theatre are also suited to type D.[2]

It is true of almost any building that its solid form lives on, long after the purpose for which it was designed has died; in the theatre this is particularly true. Provision must be made for a building which, while satisfying the needs of the present, will not hinder the developments of the future more than can be helped. The present building tendency towards the use of machine-made prefabricated units should help here, and more use could be made in theatre design of this style of building, so that the theatre may change its clothing

[1] An example of type A, drawings and photographs for the Oxford University Theatre, will be found in *Oxford Drama Commission's Report on the American Theatre*, Oxford University Press, 1948. Also in: Architect's Journal, October 28 and November 4, 1948.

[2] The requirements of types D and E are fully covered in *The Essentials of Stage Planning* by Stanley Bell, Norman Marshall and Richard Southern, for the British Drama League, Frederick Muller, 1949.

from time to time both easily and cheaply; the theatre building should be as alive and capable of growth as the drama which it enshrines.

Whereas the use of the auditorium is not likely to change to any great extent during the lifetime of the building, it is possible that the back-stage area of the theatre will need to undergo alterations to conform with new requirements in scenic design, and to this end the theatre design must be kept as simple as possible. The main point for any architect to bear always in mind is that the stage designer's most urgent requirement is uninterrupted and unlimited space, and then more uninterrupted space. Given plenty of flat stage space, a good flying system and the correct form of proscenium opening, all points which will be discussed at greater length later in the book, I contend that any form of play can be adequately mounted without the need for the provision of any complicated machinery. In order to arrive at this open stage space, it is best if the back-stage area is designed on a frame or grid system of supports, light prefabricated units being used for filling in the necessary wall spaces, so that if the need arises the whole pattern of the back-stage area can be changed at will.

4. *What is a Civic Theatre?*

IN THIS BOOK it is assumed that promoters of the civic
theatre appreciate that a building which is designed to
function adequately as a theatre cannot be used to serve any
other purpose.[1] Far too many civic bodies have supposed
that the provision of a multi-purpose hall will satisfy the
need for a theatre in their city, and, while this may once have
been the case if such a civic hall were intended only for
occasional use by amateur dramatic companies, it does not
even begin to meet the requirements of a permanent professional repertory company. It is the provision of a permanent
home for such a company, made possible by recent legisla-
tion, that we are considering in this book. Unfortunately, as
we shall show later, a building which is properly suited to its
use as a theatre would be quite useless as a dance-hall or
concert hall, the reverse being equally true. The drama requires to be housed in its own particular type of building if
it is to produce worthwhile results.

What is meant by the term 'Civic Theatre'? This is the
name generally applied to a theatre which, provided by civic
or individual enterprise, is run on professional non-profit-
making lines to provide a high standard of drama for the
citizens of the city or town. Unlike the ordinary commercial
theatre, its function is to provide for the artistic needs of the
community in the sphere of drama without commercial profit:
such profits as are made by any particular play, over and
above the running costs of the theatre, are used to provide for
better productions in the future. Although such a theatre
may be started with the aid of a grant, it will be expected to

[1] *Design for a Civic Theatre* by Richard Leacroft; New Theatre, August
1947. For a definition of the scope and purpose of Civic Theatres see *The
British Drama League Civic Theatre Scheme,* also the text of the *Local Govern-
ment Act,* 1948, section 132, Dobson's Theatre Year-Book, 1948–9, pp.
395–412, Dennis Dobson, 1948.

be self-supporting once it has become established. From this it is clear that, whereas it is still commercially sound in that it has to pay its own way, it is able, because its profits can be used to pay for productions of high artistic merit which are not necessarily pot-boilers, to perform a greater range of plays than the commercial repertory theatre which must limit its choice to such plays as have already proved box-office successes. Among other plays the civic theatre will be expected to produce, from time to time, those having an educational value, including such obvious choices as the School Certificate play of the year.

In order to pay its way, the theatre company will need to perform a large number of plays which will attract the public in sufficient numbers to provide the running costs of theatre and company as a minimum requirement: this means that they will not be able, even if they so wished, to concentrate on performing only experimental plays. To maintain a constant appeal to the limited audience of a provincial town it is necessary to produce plays either on the 'repertory' or on the 'repertoire' principle. In the repertory type a different play is produced every two or three weeks; in the repertoire type the company first rehearses some half-dozen plays which are then performed on different nights of the week, new plays being introduced into, or failures dropped from, the repertoire as required. The architect will need to know which arrangement is most likely to be used in the theatre, as it will affect the design of the stores and workshops. This aspect of the problem will be studied in greater detail when the appropriate portions of the building are being considered.

In addition to the work described above, the civic theatre may well form the nucleus of a county drama scheme, touring versions of the plays performed at the central theatre being produced in the central rehearsal rooms and workshops before touring the village halls (theatre type E) of the county districts, the audiences of which are unable to reach the central theatre. It might be decided to run drama courses at the theatre for full-time students in conjunction with the local University or College: in this case the provision of a number of lecture rooms and a small experimental theatre would probably be required.[2] This again will call for special requirements in the design and these are all points about which the architect should be prepared to inquire, and which the sponsors of the scheme should tabulate before they consider building.

As it will be necessary to perform some twenty or thirty plays a year in the theatre, and it is unlikely that this number of new plays will be written each year of a quality good enough to justify the production risk unavoidable in such cases, it follows that the theatre company will need to perform a fair number of established plays and revivals.[3] It may therefore be safely assumed that the present-day naturalistic or semi-naturalistic box-set form of play will need to be catered for in the building, and this will naturally affect the plan. It may also be necessary to perform plays of past ages with a certain amount of verisimilitude, but this is not an all-important factor in this form of theatre, and is better provided for in the theatre of type A.

So much for the present and the past. What of the future? Can the form of the play of the future be assessed with any certainty? The general tendency in the British theatre has been towards intimacy of production, with an off-shoot towards spectacle when the use of naturalistic scenery was in its hey-day. In general, however, the play has tended to concentrate on the spoken word and on the actor-audience contact. Where experimental plays have been performed they have had to rely on small theatres as their places of production, as it has not been safe to hazard an unknown type of play on the West End stage which has the monopoly of the large theatres. Has this fact affected the style of the plays?

[2] See *London Theatre Studio*, Architects' Journal, July 29, 1937. *A.D.C. Theatre, Cambridge*, Architect and Building News, January 25, 1935.

[3] For a general indication of the variety of plays and settings found in repertory theatre work, see: *Adventure in Repertory* by Aubrey Dyas, Northampton Repertory Players, 1948. Also *Birmingham Repertory Theatre* by Thomas C. Kemp, Cornish Brothers Ltd., 1943.

Would they have been conceived on a different or larger scale if there had been any chance of a large theatre being available? It is safe to say that where experiments have been made their general tendency has been towards a greater contact between the audience and the actor, and has been away from the spectacular production, which form of drama is now well provided for by the films. It is constantly asserted by the dramatists that if they had a new form of theatre provided for them they would be able to write a new form of play, but until this play is conceived it is an extremely difficult task to provide a suitable theatre: a vicious circle! There has, in recent years, been a great revival of interest in music and the ballet, and it must be allowed that the play of the future may well incorporate these elements, and that the latter may bring with it a revived interest in the 'painted form' of scenery usually associated with ballet, and consisting of wings set at

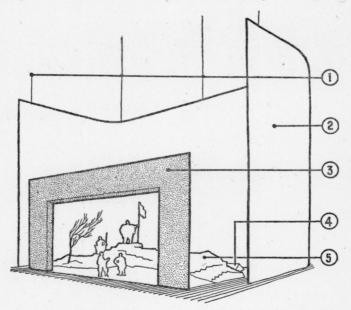

Fig. 10. Diagram illustrating cyclorama setting

1, lines from grid. 2, cyclorama or sky-cloth. 3, inner or false proscenium. 4, lighting units. 5, three-dimensional scenery.

the sides of the stage, the whole stage being dominated by one large backcloth. It may be that the formation of these civic theatres will encourage the rebirth of the self-contained theatre group which writes its own plays to suit its own players.

Scenery has progressed from the traditional painted scene, through a tide of naturalism to the present-day built-up set. It now wavers between the fully-built naturalistically painted setting, the abstract architectural setting, and the form provided by a few essential properties set before curtains or a cyclorama, together with the use of experimental lighting. The introduction of the ballet type of scenery into straight plays may mean the re-introduction of a form of scenery based more on painting than on architecture.

The effect of these various forms of settings on the stage plan will be examined when that portion of the theatre is being considered. At present the lack of materials necessary for the scenic art has forced a certain simplification on the settings, and this, if it continues, may well affect the structure of the new plays. Will the present conventions remain, or may we return to a state where the scenes are once again changed in full view of the audience? The answer to this and other questions raised will decide the equipment which we must provide in the new civic theatre. Unfortunately the theatre is one place where fads and fashions are in their element, and what is preached today is condemned tomorrow. Care must therefore be taken in the choice of theatre form, to see that the new building which provides for the current fashion, be it 'space' play or other form, will not be transformed into a white elephant by the passage of time. It would be as well to take a long term view, and to take into account the traditions of the past, when attempting to formulate views on the future.

c

5. *Site Planning and Restrictions*

APART FROM THE restrictions imposed by the production of the plays themselves, there are a number of outside restrictions which will tend to limit the design. These may be referred to briefly under the headings of site restrictions and local authorities' rules and regulations regarding the protection of the public.[1]

In many cities and towns, plans for future developments have already been worked out, and the replanning of the cities and of their civic centres is now an accomplished paper fact. This means that a space may have been set aside for development as a civic theatre. In many cases, unfortunately, the need for such a book as this is made abundantly clear, in that the sites chosen are often completely inappropriate to the use they are intended to serve. The special requirements of a civic repertory theatre, as differing from those of the normal contemporary 'West End' theatre or the more usual civic assembly hall, are not fully understood. An example taken at random may serve to illustrate the point: this scheme for a new civic centre provides for a civic theatre, and even goes so far as to show in model form the proposed building which might be erected on the site. The site chosen, however, is a restricted island site, and the scheme in no way provides for the large amount of back-stage space which is an essential part of any modern repertory theatre, and without which the theatre would not be able to perform its function adequately. The sites chosen for the future theatres have, in many cases,

---

[1] *Manual of Safety Requirements in Theatres and places of Public Entertainment*, Home Office, 1934. *Summary of the Home Office Manual*, 1944. *Architect's Journal Library of Planned Information* by Sir John Burnet, Tait and Lorne, extracts from the *Home Office Manual*, sheets nos. 385, 410, 419, 425, 433, 449. *L.C.C. Places of Public Entertainment*, Regulations and Rules, No. 3399, Price 1s, 1939. See also sections entitles: *Planning the small theatre* by Henry Elder, A.R.I.B.A., p. 211. *Licensing of theatre buildings*, p. 388, in Dobson's Theatre Year-Book, 1948–49, Dennis Dobson, 1948.

been selected by persons unacquainted with theatrical requirements, and the architect who may eventually be called
upon to design a theatre on such a site will find himself unnecessarily hampered by restrictions inherent in the inappropriate site, with the result that the design of the theatre will
suffer, and may even prove to be quite useless for its special
purpose.

While there is still plenty of time before any building
operations can commence, civic authorities must be warned
of these dangers, and should be encouraged to reconsider
their schemes in the light of modern needs.

The second form of restrictions, those laid down in their
bye-laws by the local authorities, were originally framed to
protect the public from the risk of fire in the traditional timber theatres erected on close town sites, and were further
extended to include health regulations when the commercial
managements attempted, in their new buildings, to provide
for the maximum number of paying customers on the minimum area of site.

The civic theatre of the future, while still situated amidst
the hustle and bustle of ordinary every-day life, should de-
finitely be planned with a view to adding to the recreational
amenities of the city or town. With this point in mind, the
site chosen should be in some pleasant open space near the
centre of the town, which can be provided with gardens:
thereby adding to the lunch-time amenities of sandwich-eating
citizens, while at the same time ensuring that the theatre is
always in their thoughts. If some such open space is not already available, then the site chosen should be large enough
to enable the theatre building to be designed with some civic
dignity. If possible it should form part of an entertainment
centre, and might be grouped with such buildings as the
Museum, Art Gallery and Library, and the addition of an
open-air theatre would be an added advantage. It is realized
that it will not be possible to choose such sites in every town
which requires a civic theatre, but it is an ideal solution which
is envisaged here, and every effort should be made to ap-

proach as nearly as possible to this solution in each individual instance.

In many provincial cities and towns it is extremely difficult for the citizen to provide his family and himself with a reasonable evening meal before going to the theatre. Late working hours, early theatre performances and early closing of restaurants account for this difficulty, and in many cases the home is too far distant from the place of work to allow for a comfortable journey there and to the theatre with a

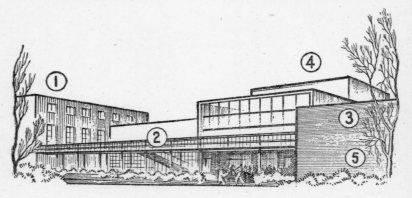

Fig. 11. A civic entertainment centre for a small town

1, library. 2, museum with art gallery over. 3, restaurant and tea-terrace. 4, civic theatre. 5, hall or rehearsal room.

meal between. Bearing these points in mind, the new theatres should provide all things necessary for an evening's entertainment: a good tea-room and restaurant, plenty of lounge facilities, and space for exhibitions and other means of passing the time until the play is due to start. It should be possible for the average citizen to go straight from his work to the theatre, where he may meet his friends or relatives waiting for him in the lounge. They may have a good, but cheap, meal, and spend the time until the play begins looking at the exhibitions or, in fine weather, taking the air reclining in comfortable chairs on the terraces overlooking the gardens.

If the theatre is planned on these lines, on a site where there is room to spread the buildings without cramping one department on top of another, and where sufficient exits from the stage and auditorium can be provided direct to the open air, then the local authority may be persuaded to relax some of its more stringent requirements, which in many cases exert a strangle-hold on any attempt to provide a theatre more suited to present-day requirements than those traditional forms on built-up sites which gave birth to the rules and regulations, and which no longer answer the needs of the new theatre with its greatly extended scenic requirements.

Before leaving the question of site planning it would be as well to include a warning against preconceived ideas on the part of either the theatre client or the architect. To provide an example: it would seem, from a close study of the various block-plans of the first six designs submitted in the competition for the Stratford-on-Avon Memorial Theatre, that the early idea of the promoters of the scheme, the linking of the stage of the new theatre with the remains of the old theatre, was the main stumbling block to the vision of the competing architects. This requirement seems to have been the main factor in determining the size of the stage, resulting in the very cramped space, since enlarged but still insufficient, which is so apparent the moment one enters the back-stage area during the run of a season. If this limiting factor had been dispensed with, it is very likely that the planning of the stage on more open lines would have resulted.[2]

[2] See *Shakespeare Memorial Theatre, Stratford-on-Avon* by G. A. Jellicoe, Ernest Benn, 1933. The Architect and Building News, 22 April 1932, 23 June 1933. *The Other Theatre* by Norman Marshall, John Lehmann, 1947, p. 175.

6. *The Theatre Building*

WHAT IS MEANT by the term 'theatre'? The word really comprehends the whole realm of dramatic expression. We are concerned here with the building in which this expression comes to life. In the theatre building are two complementary groups of people: the actors and the audience. The relationship between these two groups is relatively simple: the one group should perform and act, the other should see and hear. The building affects directly and vitally the relationship between these two groups as the historical section has endeavoured to show.

In the early theatre forms, the circus (Fig. 1), the classic theatre (Fig. 2), the pageant stage (Fig. 3), and the Elizabethan theatre (Fig. 4), this relationship was clearly and truthfully expressed. The early Restoration theatre (Fig. 5) maintained this relationship, but from this time forward, as we have seen, two factors were added to the design of theatre buildings which complicated the direct relationship. These were the desire to accommodate a much larger audience, and the need to provide for scenery. The final outcome of the addition of these factors was the development of a theatre building (Fig. 6) which no longer provided an adequate expression of the primary relationship considered above, but which vitally affected that relationship by the nature of the physical features dictated by the acceptance of these new requirements.

The desire for commercial profits which led theatre managers in the past to alter the size and shape of the theatres from the workable primary plan, is a feature which should be absent from the new civic theatres; it should therefore be possible to limit the numbers in the audience and by this means limit the size of the auditorium to one which will provide for the necessary intimacy inherent in the primary relationship. This intimacy may be defined as the identifying of the playgoer with the emotion and movement of the play and of the performers, from moment to moment, in a manner so close that he feels himself to be literally committed to the outcome of the plot as though he were personally involved, for it cannot be too strongly emphasized that in the theatre the audience make as essential a contribution to the production as do the actors.

The return to the primary circus form of theatre has been envisaged in suggested designs for new theatres, but, while these forms are feasible when the designs of experimental theatres of type A are being considered, they will not fully answer the problems of a civic theatre. As we noted in section 4, provision must be made not only for the production of contemporary plays, but also for the plays of past ages, and since these plays were all designed to suit the requirements of the particular form of theatre then in use, it follows that the civic theatre must make allowance for this fact. Whatever the demerits of the picture-frame stage, the box-set form of play is an integral part of it, and if we are to provide for this type of production, then our new theatre must necessarily allow for the masking requirements of the box-set, and the arrangement of the audience in the auditorium must be so related to the stage as to allow all persons to see the entire performance. These arrangements would obviously be impossible in the circus theatre, since such a scene may be viewed from one side only, and half of the auditorium would be behind the set; in addition, most local authorities will require that it should be possible to separate the scenery from the audience by a fire-resisting barrier.

These various scenic requirements have all imposed their restrictions on the actor-audience relationship and must now be taken into account, together with all the advances that have been made in lighting and scenic machinery. The form of the new civic theatre must be based on contemporary design, but every effort must be made to arrange the necessary elements in such a way that as many different theatre forms as possible may be included in the one building. Should the play of the future require a stage completely open to the audience, then it must be possible to remove whatever masking elements may lie between; at the same time provision must be made for the actor to perform within the limits of the auditorium in the manner of the Shakespearian or Restoration theatres, surrounded by his audience.

Scenic effects may be achieved by many and varied methods: a lone actor may appear on the flat stage area set against a cyclorama suggesting infinite distance; coloured lights on abstract scenery may provide quick and noiseless changes of scene, or many yards of painted canvas may be required to represent the locale. All forms of setting should be possible on the new stage, but whatever form is used the essential functions are the same: to set the place or the 'mood' and to provide the necessary variations in level of the acting area. If these scenic variations can once again form part of the structure of the theatre and of the auditorium as they did in the early forms of theatre, then a closer link may be formed with the audience than if these levels were all confined, as they are today, behind a proscenium arch. The provision of fore-stages, side-stages, stage doors and stage boxes required for the performance of plays of the past, will at the same time allow for the needs of the future. The auditorium and stage must form a single unit in the presentation of a play; no longer may they remain separate entities connected only by a 'hole in the wall', the auditorium must once again provide the players with their various acting levels and entrances.

In the remainder of the book we will now proceed to see how these requirements can be satisfied.

7. The Stage

THE STAGE OF a contemporary theatre is divided into two
main sections:

1. *The acting area*: the area on which the action of the
play takes place in view of the audience.

2. *The working area*: the area used for the storage of
scenery and furniture, and for the assembly of actors prior
to their appearance on the acting area. This area should not
be visible to the audience.

(a) THE ACTING AREA

The ideal shape for the acting area is a flat rectangular
surface. As plays of all types and periods will be performed
in a civic theatre, provision must be made for their proper
presentation, but an historically accurate reconstruction of
the original style of performance is not possible without an
exact replica of the building for which they were designed.
In a civic theatre this is not necessary as this form of presentation would have little, if any, appeal to the majority of the
audience, who wish to see the plays performed according to
the conventions to which they are accustomed, making use
of modern stage equipment. The scholarly reconstructions
would be played in the experimental theatres of type A,
which are especially designed for them. In the civic theatre
it is necessary to provide only an approximation of the actor-
audience relationship essential to each type of production.

The characteristics of the acting areas of the Classic,
Elizabethan, Restoration and Georgian theatres have already
been noted. The main essential of all these theatres is a fore-
stage, or stage set within the limits of the auditorium, and it
is obvious that something of this sort must be provided in
the new theatre. The box-set type of presentation, however,
can only be adequately presented on the main stage, and the

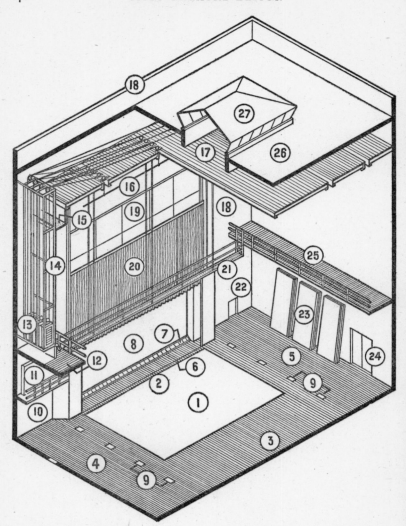

Fig. 12. Diagram illustrating the parts of a contemporary stage

1, acting area. 2, down-stage. 3, up-stage. 4, prompt-side wing. 5, O.P. side wing. 6, carpet cut. 7, footlights. 8, proscenium opening. 9, electric dips. 10, stage manager's corner. 11, electrician's gallery and switch-board. 12, fly-gallery—working side. 13, counter-weights. 14, counter-weight tracks. 15, loading gallery. 16, barrel. 17, grid. 18, proscenium wall. 19, safety curtain. 20, front curtain. 21, lighting bridge. 22, door to panatrope room. 23, scenery packs. 24, door to scene dock. 25, fly-gallery. 26, fire-resisting roof. 27, haystack lantern.

ideal shape of its acting area is a flat rectangular surface with its main axis at right angles to the majority of the audience, who view the play from one side only through the proscenium opening which masks the working areas of the stage. If, however, for the demands of the period plays, a large fore-stage is built out in front of the proscenium, the difficulty arises that the distance between the actor, playing in a box-set, and the audience seated beyond the fore-stage is too great for the intimate relationship which must be established between them: it will therefore be necessary to provide for the easy removal of the fore-stage when it is not required by the nature of the production.

As stated, the ideal acting area should be flat. There would seem to be a belief common among architects that a sloping floor to the stage is essential to give the audience good sight-lines, but this is not so. The sloping stage is the last lingering remains of the back-stage portion of the Restoration theatre, which accommodated the vistas of perspective scenery, the floor being sloped to help the effect of perspective. The presence of a sloping stage in a modern theatre means that the scenery for even the simplest form of set must be specially built if it is to stand vertically on the stage. Unless this is done the whole room will lean precariously towards the audience, and pictures, candelabra, etc., will call attention to this by hanging in their normal vertical positions. A sloping stage is a decided disadvantage if trucks, revolves and other methods of moving scenery are to be used.

Trucks, or wagons, are low platforms some 3 in. to 6 in. high, mounted on castors and capable of being pushed to any part of the stage. Heavy scenery may be built on them and thus be easily moved from one point to another. If used on a sloping stage, however, they are liable to get out of hand and run away down the slope.

A revolve is usually in the form of a circular platform, it is used for the same purpose as a revolving stage, but while the latter is level with, and part of, the stage proper, the former is mounted on castors and stands on the stage. When set on a sloping stage it is liable to jam.

It can therefore be said that the sloping stage creates more problems than it solves, and the question of sight-lines can be dealt with quite simply by ramping or sloping the floor of the auditorium.

The acting area may need to be extended in depth to provide either for the perspective vista type of scenery required by a Restoration play, or for the use of a cyclorama—a cove of canvas or plaster, which, when correctly lit, gives an impression of distance. The cyclorama needs to be placed well to the rear of the acting area so that light used to illumine the actors will not spill on to it, thereby spoiling the effect (see section 9 (*b*)).

While still on the question of the acting area consideration must be given to the need for bridges or traps cut in the stage floor. It has been seen how, in the traditional British theatre, the floor of the stage was divided into various sections, which moved and allowed for the raising of scenery and performers. Later the stage was divided into sections which rose or fell by mechanical means to give a variety of acting levels. To what extent is it necessary to provide such machinery in the new theatre? We have seen that the bridges and sliders of the traditional theatre became redundant on the introduction of the present form of scenery, and their re-introduction would be of little practical value; as the funds available for building a civic theatre are probably somewhat limited, the additional expense involved by the introduction of the mechanically operated stage sections would not be worth the results obtained. It must, however, be possible to take up or remove any portion of the acting area to form a trap or opening in the floor, wherever the action of the play may so require; for this purpose the stage floor and supporting joists should be designed in removable sections which can be taken up and replaced at will. It should be noted here that some local authorities may have bye-laws governing the design of the stage floor: the L.C.C. require that the stage floor should be of hard-

wood not less than 1¼ in. thick. Some theatres provide a linoleum covering to the stage, and this is in many ways an excellent finish as it allows for easy painting, washing and cleaning. Its only drawbacks, as a permanent covering, are that
it must be laid in sections to correspond to the removable
portions of the stage, and it is easily damaged, particularly
near the edges, when scenery is moved across it. Other
theatres use a stage cloth, or canvas covering, laid over the
bare boards. This may be plain or it may be painted as the
scene demands; its use, however, calls for the addition of
a carpet cut, or narrow hinged trap in the floor of the stage
(see Figs. 9 and 12), which runs the full width of the acting
area, and is placed directly behind the front curtain. The
front edge of the stage cloth is dropped into this opening
and held in place by the cover which is closed down and traps
the cloth. Whichever form of stage covering is used it would
be as well to provide a carpet cut. In front of this should be
a similar trap, which when opened will reveal footlights, and
when these are not required can be shut down to provide a
level stage, as, for instance, when the built-out fore-stage is
in use.

(b) THE WORKING AREA

If the present methods of staging a play are to continue,
then a working area must be provided around the acting
area.

What are these methods, and how do they affect the design
of the theatre? As hinted earlier in the book, back-stage
methods are something of a mystery to the average layman,
and for the sake of the architect it will be necessary to des-
cribe briefly how a set is built, presented and changed during
a performance.

Scenery is normally composed of canvas screens or 'flats'
(see Fig. 9) which average some 4 ft. to 6 ft. wide by 16 ft.
to 18 ft. high. On these flats are painted portions of the walls
of the rooms, etc., and, where necessary, doors, windows and
fireplaces are let into them. These flats are cleated, or lashed,

together with lines and cleats to form the walls of the room or set. They are held firmly in place by metal or wood braces which may be attached to the back, and which are weighted or screwed to the floor. If there is more than one setting in the play the designer tries to plan his sets so that the main setting becomes a 'standing' set and the remainder are arranged as 'insets'. These insets are planned, as their name implies, to fit inside the standing set, and it is therefore necessary to 'strike', i.e. remove, only such parts of the standing set as will allow for the entry and setting up of the flats forming the inset. When a scene is finished the stage hands strike the set. To do this they unlash the flats and 'run' each one separately to a 'pack' against a nearby wall (see Fig. 12), i.e. they are leant one on top of another against the wall in the order in which they will next be needed. The rear wall of the set consisting of several flats may well have been battened-out to form one unit, and in this case it may then be 'flown', complete, into the air (see Section 9). When a ceiling is used with a box-set this is usually in the form of a large rectangle of canvas on a timber frame somewhat larger in size than the biggest setting is likely to be. It is hung in a horizontal position from two sets of lines, one set at the front edge and one at the rear. When the set is in use the ceiling is allowed to rest on the tops of the flats, and whenever a scene-change is to be made this ceiling must be raised to allow the flats to be moved (see Figs. 6 and 9). As soon as a space has been formed in the wall of the set, the furnishings are removed from the acting area, and are stored in some convenient position, the new dressings for the next set are then placed on the stage, and these are followed by the scenery which is cleated into position, and the ceiling once again dropped into place.

From this brief description it will be seen that a considerable space is needed around the acting area, where several packs and built-up pieces of scenery may be stored, furniture and properties placed ready for immediate use, effects worked, and where actors may congregate before making their entrances. It also implies that a convenient wall-space must be provided on either side of the stage where scene packs may be made, and it will further be seen that the distance through which each piece of scenery may be moved should be as short as possible so as to economize in labour and time; the essence of any scene change being great speed.

All this means that a really skilled band of stage hands is needed to strike and reset as quickly, efficiently and quietly as possible. Unfortunately really skilled theatre workers are becoming increasingly hard to find, and although in a permanent theatre it should be possible to train men to the required level of proficiency, it seems that it is hard even to find men willing to be trained. Apart from the fact that the work is arduous and the hours long and difficult, this is largely due to the present system of casual employment and payment which makes the work of the stage crew merely a part-time job which they perform in addition to earning an outside living wage.

From my own experience in the repertory theatre I have found it increasingly necessary to build as many sets as possible in advance, thereby reducing the amount of actual 'setting' during the play to an absolute minimum. This was usually accomplished by building the standing set in the normal way on the stage, and the insets in advance on trucks, the strike thereby being limited to the movement of some furniture and carpets, and the striking of two flats from one side of the standing set to allow space for the entry of the inset. By this means the members of the full-time back-stage staff are kept fully employed during their morning hours of work in the weeks of preparation.

When all the sets are built on trucks or wagons, complete with their own ceiling and all their dressings (see Fig. 28), then the change during the show is limited to the removal of one truck and its replacement by another, a movement which can be accomplished by a comparatively unskilled crew. Incidentally, the number of night staff required to work the show may be reduced by these methods, resulting in a substantial saving in wages. It is recalled that this is no innovation in the British theatre, but with the exception of the Stratford Memorial Theatre—which has built-in sliding sections of stage which accomplish somewhat the same purpose, but are naturally more costly to install—no theatre in Britain has been built especially to cater for this type of production. Where trucks have been used the theatres have, in many cases, been quite unsuited to their use, many of the West End stages even retaining their rakes.

Here then are two methods of changing scenery at present in use in the contemporary theatre, and while it is not essential that the new theatre shall make use of the latter method of mounting its scenery, the architect must make sure that sufficient space is provided so that the system would work should it be employed at any future date.

Before proceeding further a few more stage terms must be explained, so that the architect may fully understand the descriptions which follow. In the traditional theatre the stage sloped up away from the footlights, and so when we walk away from the audience we speak of going *up-stage*, and when towards the audience, of going *down-stage*. When standing on the stage facing the audience, the side of the stage on our left-hand side is known as the *Prompt side*, and on our right-hand is known as the *O.P.* or *Opposite Prompt*. The areas directly on either side of the acting area are called the *Wings*, and the area over the stage is known as the *Flies* or *Flying space* (see Fig. 12).

8. *The Stage in Plan*

As most local authorities require that the stage and the scenery should be separated from the audience by a fire-resisting wall and curtain, the main acting area will necessarily be placed directly behind this wall, known as the proscenium wall, which separates the stage from the auditorium. What will be the size of the main acting area, and where will the rear and side walls of the stage be placed in relation to it?

An ideal width for the contemporary form of box setting is 30 ft., and an average depth is from 16 to 20 ft. to the rear wall of the room, with a further 5 to 10 ft. behind this for halls, gardens, etc., making in all an acting area 30 ft. wide by 25 to 30 ft. deep. When scenery is to be struck and packed against the side walls, the width of the wings, while allowing sufficient space for the packs and for the movement of furniture and actors, must not be too great or the scenery will have to be run unnecessary distances between set and pack. A distance of half the width of the acting area is ample allowance on either side, in the case of a 30 ft. wide acting area this would be 15 ft. making in all a total width to the stage of 60 ft. Up-stage of the main acting area there must be provision for a 'no-man's-land' of some 15 to 20 ft. in depth before reaching the position of the cyclorama, and behind this a further 5 ft. to allow for the passage of actors from one side of the stage to the other, and also to provide space for the storage of scenery: making in all a total depth from proscenium wall to rear wall of between 50 and 60 ft. The total stage space must be completely open, and must not be interrupted by pillars, columns, piers or walls, there must be no projections from the walls and any necessary fittings must be built-in flush to present a smooth wall surface. The stage should be directly connected to the workshop area by an opening 10 to 12 ft. wide by 25 ft. high; this opening should

D

be fitted with a fire-resisting door or sliding shutter (see Fig. 13).

If the movement of scenery is to be effected on trucks, however, then this stage space must be increased, and allowance must be made for the use of a number of trucks of varying sizes. These may be used either as separate units or fixed together to take an entire setting; they will be mounted on noiseless castors and will be free to run in whatever direction may be required. (The built-in sliding stage permits only lateral movement in its simplest form.) The units will be placed on whatever part of the stage may be required

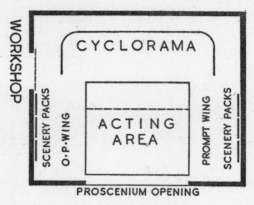

Fig. 13. Stage plan for use with scene packs

by the action of the play, or may even be used to serve the purpose of a revolving stage.

To calculate the size of the areas required for the movement of such trucks, it would be well to work to the maximum sizes that are ever likely to be used, and it should therefore be assumed that the movement of an entire setting occupying an area of 30 ft. wide by 20 ft. deep might be a feasible proposition. Sufficient space in the wings should therefore be allowed for a composite truck of this size to be run off on one side or the other. Although the furnishings of the various sets would mainly be left in position on the trucks, there will be a certain amount of movement of furniture, proper-

ties, actors and staff in the wing spaces, and it should therefore be possible to run a truck well off to one side and still
allow space for this movement around the acting area. This
wing space should be in the nature of 6 to 10 ft. wide, making
a total width for the stage of from 42 to 50 ft. On either side,
beyond the limits of the stage proper, bays should be provided to receive the trucks. These bays should be deep
enough to provide for two sets to stand on their trucks side
by side, one up-stage of the other, ready for moving into
position on the stage. Each bay will need to be from 32 to
35 ft. wide by 45 ft. deep, and the whole depth of each bay

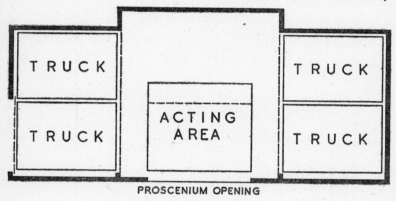

Fig. 14. Stage plan for use with trucks

should be open to the stage. One of these bays must connect
directly with the carpenter's and painter's workshops, which
in turn should connect with the scene stores (see Fig. 14).

This arrangement would not, however, allow sufficient
space in the wings should it be required to pack scenery instead of using trucks, and in fact in this arrangement there
would be no side walls on which to build the packs, except
right up-stage, as the side walls of the stage are open to the
truck bays to a depth of 45 ft.

A compromise must be found which will allow for either
form of scene movement being used, and at the same time
reduce the size of the stage to proportions which are more

likely to fit in with the financial situation. An adequate
arrangement would be to design one side of the stage to
allow sufficient width for the normal packing of scenery,
with perhaps an extra width for the occasional storage in this
space of a small truck. The width then on one side would be
from 15 to 20 ft., the latter measurement being the maximum distance through which it would be advisable to run
scenery. As will be seen later, it would be best to plan this
wing on the prompt side of the stage, but if through site

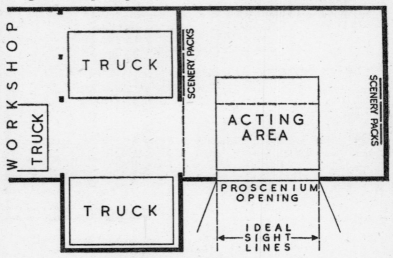

Fig. 15. Stage plan for use with scene packs or trucks

restrictions this layout cannot be followed, then the following
layout may be reversed. In fact there is no reason why the
prompt corner should not be correspondingly transferred to
the opposite side of the theatre, in this case all later recom-
mendations as to the positions of the various shops, offices,
and dressing rooms should be correspondingly reversed. The
O.P. side of the stage may now be planned as for the truck
bay design, with a wing space of 10 ft. and a truck bay
beyond. If possible the plan should be so arranged as to
allow space for packing scenery on the O.P. side of the stage
against the rear of the proscenium wall in the wing space,

or against the side wall of the stage, up-stage of the opening leading to the truck bay. This opening need only be wide enough to allow for the passage of one truck 20 ft. wide. The trucks can then run straight from the acting area, through the truck bay and into the workshop. Space for manouvring and storing the trucks will now need to be planned on either side of this 'passage way', and an area the width of the bay, 32 to 35 ft. wide by 22 to 25 ft. deep, should be allowed on the up- and down-stage sides of the bay. If this arrangement is carried out it should be possible to use, if required at any time, three trucks, each the size of a full set, which can be placed on the stage in any order, including repetitions of the same set. Should a particular play call for the use of more than three full scenes, then it must be possible for one set to be dismantled and be replaced by another setting while the play proceeds. Although this would normally be carried out in the workshop area there should be reasonable access from the scene stores to the truck bays (see Fig. 15).

To provide for an acting area of 30 ft. width we therefore have a stage some 50 to 60 ft. deep from proscenium wall to rear wall and 60 ft. wide between side walls; if, however, the proscenium opening and acting area are increased in width, the width of the whole stage will vary accordingly. The front, or 'setting line', of a set placed on the acting area will be several feet up-stage from the proscenium wall, the intermediate distance being occupied by a safety curtain, front curtain and false or inner proscenium. This distance must be kept as small as possible. It will be realized, however, that the down-stage edge of the opening in the O.P. wall leading to the truck bay will necessarily line through with this setting line so as to provide a straight run through for the trucks. While dealing with the question of the opening from the stage to the truck bay, it should be remembered that the local authority may well require that the bay and workshops should be separated from the stage, and from one another, by a fire-resisting door of one form or another, which would best be arranged as a counter-weighted shutter similar to the fire curtain.[1] The use of roller shutters is liable to prove excessively noisy, especially if it should be necessary to operate them during a performance. The need for such doors, and the provision of other fire precautions is, however, a point which the individual architect must determine for himself in his own particular area. If such a shutter is provided, it would be as well to provide an additional pass door between the stage and the bay.

One extremely important point, which cannot be too strongly stressed when dealing with this particular portion of the theatre, is the fact that the stage, the side bays, the workshops, the storage space and the loading dock platform must all have floors at the same level, and it is absolutely essential that there should be no ramps, steps or differences of level of any sort or form between these various sections. It is only on a completely level floor throughout that the necessary stage movements can be carried out with the speed and complete fluidity necessary for the easy and competent running of any show.

While dealing with the actual working areas of the stage, it will be as well to mention the need to set aside an area directly behind the proscenium wall on the prompt side of the stage for the use of the Stage Director and of the Prompter. The space allotted may be designed as an enclosed area approximately 3 ft. wide by 6 to 9 ft. long, capable of being rendered both light and sound proof, and at the same time allowing for the greatest possible view both of the acting area and of the wing space. Here will be provided the necessary telephonic and cue-light communications with the various working areas of the stage and of the front-of-house. In addition, provision should be made here for the installation of an electric clock, and for the release mechanism operating the safety curtain. This is the nerve centre of the theatre, as the stage director is responsible for the smooth running of the entire show. It should control the entrance to the stage both from the dressing rooms, so that the stage manager may

[1] See *Home Office Manual*, 1934, section 73.

easily assemble and check the actors, and also from the front-of-house (see Section 12 (*e*)).

If doors are to be placed in the rear wall of the stage they should be placed outside the limits of the acting area as projected back to the rear wall. At the same time it is worth noting that the L.C.C. rules and regulations require that . . . 'an exit shall be provided from each side of the stage and one of such exits shall lead direct to a thoroughfare or way through an unventilated lobby constructed of fire-resisting materials with self-closing fire-resisting doors hung to open in the direction of exit and fitted with automatic fastenings only'.[2]

[2] See *Home Office Manual*, 1934, sections 16–18.

9. *The Stage in Section*

FLYING SPACE ABOVE the stage is as important a feature of our contemporary theatre as it was in those of the past, and it may well be that the theatre of the future will require a similar flying system. The architect who does not allow for this possibility in the design of a new theatre is unnecessarily restricting both the use of the stage space and of the scenic effects which can be devised on it. The provision of some kind of system for hanging or flying scenery above the stage is essential in any theatre.

What is the required height of the structure over the stage area? The architect must turn, at this point, to the sections of his design to decide the exact height of the grid from which the scenery will hang. His calculations must be based on the assumption that a backcloth may be anything up to 30 ft. in its vertical dimension, and if two backcloths are hanging one behind the other, it must be possible to raise the front one to such a height as will reveal the full height of the second cloth to the audience, that is to say to a height of 60 ft. The height of the grid will, however, need to allow for the fact that in a counter-weight system the cloth may be suspended some distance below the barrel to which the wire lines are attached (see Figs. 12, 16 and 17), and it will not then be possible to raise the cloth until it actually touches the underside of the grid. An additional 3 to 4 ft. should be added to the calculated height to allow for this and other possible emergencies. A normal working height may well be in the nature of 65 to 70 ft., or even higher. A further consideration is raised by the L.C.C. requirement that there shall be sufficient height above the stage ' . . . to allow of the safety curtain being raised above the top of the proscenium opening in one piece and of all scenes being so raised without rolling'.

Above the grid sufficient height must be allowed for a man

to inspect, alter or add spot-lines to the grid in comfort; these latter lines are sometimes added to allow for the hanging or flying of scenery at points not covered by the general layout of lines. Above this will be the fire-resisting roof to the theatre with such ventilation openings, la tern-lights and sprinkler systems as may be required by the local authority.[1]

(a) THE FLYING SYSTEM

In the modern theatre the old-fashioned form of rope lines, already described, is replaced by a counter-weight system in which wire is used in place of rope, the lines at the stage end being connected to a metal barrel, and at their opposite end to a counter-weight, to which additional weights may be added to balance the weight of scenery attached to the barrel. Once the weight of the scenery to be flown has been counter-weighted, it can be raised into the air by the action of one man pulling on a working line. With a counter-weight system (see Figs. 12, 16 and 17) it is possible to fly the back wall of a set, or by using several lines to fly an entire set. It is as well, however, to provide a certain number of the old-fashioned rope lines spaced out over the area of the grid, as there are still some functions which can only be carried out with the use of a rope system.

It must be remembered that this general flying system was originally designed in the days when all scenery was set parallel with the footlights (see Fig. 7). The modern stage often requires hanging scenery set at an angle to the footlights, and if this is to be carried out on a normal flying system, one end of the scenery must be hung on an up-stage line, and the other end on a line from another set further downstage. It follows that when this diagonally-set piece of scenery is flown, it renders useless any of the sets of lines between those on which it is hung. An alternative arrangement is to hang the cloth on one set of lines in the normal manner, and then to attach a horizontal line to one end and 'brail', or pull, the scenery into the required diagonal position; neither pro-

[1] See *Home Office Manual*, 1934, sections 71, 72.

cess really answers the problem satisfactorily and it forms one of the main disadvantages of the present flying system.

For the working of the line system a fly-gallery, as described under the old-fashioned system, must be provided, and a smaller gallery must be placed directly under the level of the grid; it is used for loading and unloading the additional counter-weights. To allow for the lateral movement of scenery, which may be anything up to 20 ft. high (the standard sizes for small theatres of this kind are 16 and 18 ft.), the fly-gallery must be placed at a minimum height of 25 ft. above the stage floor. The opening between the stage and the truck bay must also be designed for the passage of scenery and a corresponding height be allowed. The working fly-gallery, i.e. the gallery from which the flying system is worked, is usually on the prompt side of the stage, this being more directly available to the stage director in case of emergency. In many theatres the fly- and loading-galleries are reached by vertical ladders up the stage walls, but it is a better arrangement if they can be approached, reasonably directly from the stage, by means of some stair or corridor surrounding the stage block. A fire exit from the galleries should be provided direct to the open air. A fly-gallery on the O.P. side of the stage will still be needed, and the two should be connected by a bridge of the cat-walk type. This bridge, placed directly up-stage of the front curtain, should be wide enough to allow for the passage of a man from one side to the other, 1 ft. to 1 ft. 6 in., and may be hung from the grid; it must be counter-weighted and be adjustable in height and may run in side tracks set between the fly-galleries and the grid, these tracks being designed in the form of vertical ladders giving access to the bridge in any position. The bridge would be used for the adjustment of lights during the performance of the play.

There are two forms of counter-weight system in use: the one-power system (see Fig. 16), in which the counter-weight travels the full height of the building, and is at stage level when the scenery is flown and vice-versa; in the second form, the two-power system (see Fig. 17), the counter-weight travels through a distance equal to half the height through which the scenery can travel. If a single-power system is used, and this is the more direct system, it would be best to arrange for the hand-brakes to be located at fly-gallery level so that the system may be worked from this point; the tracks at stage level could then be encased behind a light partition, with inspection panels for maintenance work, to enable scene packs to be made on this side of the stage. The space for the

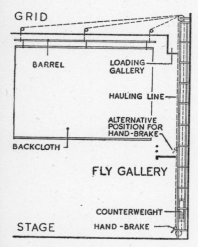

Fig. 16. A single-purchase counter-
weight system

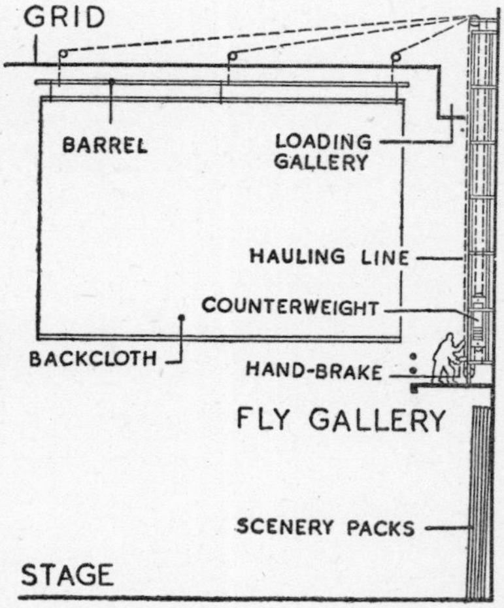

Fig. 17. A double-purchase counter-
weight system

system should be planned as an addition to the normal width of the wing. The two-power system was originally planned for use where the tracks could not be accommodated at stage level; for instance, when truck bays are required on both sides of the stage (see Fig. 14).

It is hardly necessary to point out that the grid will need to be designed to carry a very heavy loading. The architect will be able to obtain the necessary information on this point from the firms who specialize in making the required machinery.

Although machinery, other than that described directly above, may be installed if finance allows, care must be taken to ensure that such items do not in any way restrict the use of the stage space, machinery being always liable to present as many restrictions in its use as benefits. The main consideration in the design of the theatre should be to provide as flexible a stage as it is possible to conceive, and bearing this point in mind it is essential to concentrate the available financial resources on providing maximum working space rather than on expensive machinery.

(*b*) CYCLORAMA OR SKY-CLOTH

The question of the cyclorama requires special attention. There are two main forms in use today (see Fig. 10): one built solidly of fibrous plaster on a light frame; the other formed of canvas. The purpose of a cyclorama or sky-cloth is to present to the audience a perfectly smooth surface, which, when evenly lit, gives an appearance of unlimited distance and space. This effect is completely destroyed if some blemish or irregularity is allowed to appear on the surface, as this provides a point on which the 'eye' of the audience can focus, and the actual instead of the apparent distance of the cyclorama immediately becomes measurable. An ideally planned cyclorama should be of such a size that a member of the audience seated in one of the extreme side seats of the auditorium, and looking beyond the up-stage edge, or the soffit of the inner proscenium on the opposite side of the stage, can see nothing but the cyclorama beyond (see Fig. 18). This ideal arrangement, however, can seldom be carried out in actual fact, as the presence of the cyclorama tends to become an embarrassment in the rapid lateral movement of scenery, and even the possibility of flying the cyclorama at each change of scene to allow for the movement of scenery beneath is an ever-present time loser. This ideal solution should be borne in mind, however, and the best possible compromise be effected. Although a cyclorama can be used in almost any form of play, it may occasionally be found to be in the way, and as our aim is to include only such items as place the fewest restrictions on the general use of the stage area, it may be best to use the canvas variety which can be easily flown, or taken down and removed when not required. A perfectly made canvas cyclorama, properly tied off to a shaped batten at the top, and tightly laced through the bottom to eyes let into the stage, can give excellent results,

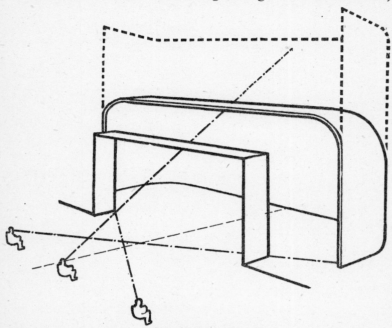

Fig. 18. Diagram illustrating alternative cyclorama designs and the use of sight-lines

especially when seen from the distances mentioned earlier in this discussion. If, however, it is decided to install a solid cyclorama then it must be possible to remove the whole structure out of the way without interfering with the use of the grid, and it must also be remembered that space must be left behind as passage way for the actors and staff so that they can pass from one side to the other without actually leaving the stage.

If a solid cyclorama is to be flown, then the overall width of the cyclorama, and especially the distance between the arms, must be greater than the width of any cloth or scenery which it may be desired to fly in the area enclosed within the three sides of the cyclorama. While the back of the cyclorama may be hung on one of the normal sets of lines, the downstage ends of the cyclorama arms must be suspended on extra spot-lines which should be placed further out from the centre line of the stage than are the remainder of the long and short lines of the system. Unless this is done it will be found that the space enclosed by the cyclorama will be unusable for the hanging and flying of scenery. This arrangement means, however, that the top of the cyclorama cannot be curved forward to match the curve of the two side arms (see Fig. 18), and the cyclorama will therefore need to be a great deal higher than would otherwise be necessary. This height may be calculated by projecting the straight line joining the nearest seat in the auditorium to the underside of the proscenium opening, and the height of the grid must be adjusted to allow for flying the cyclorama as a complete unit to allow for the movement of scenery beneath.[2] The provision of rails or tracks on which the cyclorama may run up- and down-stage, or from which it may hang, should be avoided as they tend to restrict the use of the flying area. When a canvas cyclorama is to be flown, the two arms are hinged to the back batten, and may be folded in, so that the whole cyclorama can be flown on one set of lines.

If the flat area of stage described earlier is provided, allowance made for a fore-stage, and the height over the stage raised as suggested with a flying system, then, by using trucks when required, any form of theatrical performance can be adequately presented. It is as well to emphasize again however, that the essential prime consideration in the design of a good theatre is the provision of a large area of flat

[2] See *Proscenium and Sight Lines* by Richard Southern, Faber and Faber, 1939.

workable stage, with plenty of room for the movement of cast
and scenery, and with the inclusion of only such machinery
as is unlikely to restrict the use of this area or to become redundant in the course of time.

Before continuing to examine in detail the rest of the
working areas of the stage, i.e. the workshops, dressing
rooms, green-room, etc., the other important area of the
theatre building—the auditorium—must be studied with
particular reference to its relation to the stage.

THE EXACT PHYSICAL link between the stage and the auditorium is the most important element in the theatre. In the historical section the slow movement away from the intimate atmosphere of the early theatres which culminated in the present-day picture-frame stage was noted (see Fig. 6). What are the elements of this contemporary theatre which prevent the required intimacy of production? First and foremost is the fact that the stage is set behind an ornate frame, forming the proscenium opening, which sets the actors in a world apart, and, like a picture frame, cuts them off from the audience. Secondly, the area of dead stage between the setting and the audience. A setting must necessarily be placed some 2 to 3 ft. up-stage from the proscenium wall, and while this arrangement by itself would be reasonably acceptable, the distance is often unnecessarily increased by the addition of a small permanent fore-stage or apron, which is quite useless for any practical purpose and merely helps to separate the actor from his audience. Thirdly, the distracting chasm of the sunken orchestra pit, which, with its railings, desks, lights, chairs and musicians creates virtually a physical barrier. Fourthly is the width of the front gangway. Across this barren area of dead stage, orchestra pit and gangway the actor must strive to establish contact with his audience. It would be a great deal better if the orchestra pit were entirely removed, and only a narrow gangway separated the first row of seating from the front of the stage. To reduce the amount of dead stage in front of the setting, the front edge of the stage must line through with the proscenium wall. The stage being then directly connected with the spectator, the necessary feeling of intimacy could be achieved without bringing the front row of the audience right on top of the actors: a state of affairs with which the modern actor would probably as yet, be unable to deal. This feeling of intimacy must be encouraged; it is not necessarily brought about by actual physical contact, but rather by the absence of any dividing element. The orchestra or trio must now be accommodated in some other portion of the theatre; this we will consider later.

So that the audience can see the stage as comfortably as possible the stage floor should not be designed at a greater height than 3 ft. above the floor level of the front row of seats. All members of the audience, including those in the front rows, should be able to see the actual floor of the stage and not, as in so many contemporary theatres, be able to see only down to the knees of the up-stage actors. It would be worth experimenting to see whether a stage set at a height of 2 ft. or less would help to create the intimate atmosphere

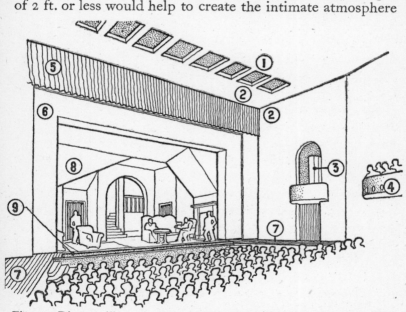

Fig. 19. Diagram illustrating the auditorium arranged for an intimate box-set production

1, grills for built-out fore-stage lighting units. 2, ceiling and walls of auditorium forming 'proscenium opening'. 3, screens covering lighting units and electrician's station in prompt-side box. 4, light units in box front. 5, front curtain. 6, adjustable inner proscenium. 7, side stages connecting stage doors to main stage. 8, box setting. 9, footlights.

between the actor and the audience. The auditorium floor should then slope or rake up from the level of the front row of seats towards the back of the house, at an angle which allows perfect vision from every seat.

The proper presentation of the intimate box-set play being now allowed for (see Fig. 19), what arrangements can be made for the proper presentation of the other forms of drama? In order to provide the choral area required for a classic play, which was situated between the raised stage and the audience, it may be necessary to remove two or three of the front rows of seating which, incidentally, may well be arranged in a slight curve, the resultant form giving a sufficient approximation to the size and shape of the required choral area. To suggest the narrow raised platform at the rear of the classic stage, and to ensure that the actors on this area are not masked by the chorus, it will probably be best to build-up the level of the stage proper by means of rostrums, the inner and upper stages of the Elizabethan style being provided in a similar manner if required; this is, however, the affair of the producer and the stage designer and will not affect the design of the theatre from the architect's point of view. The choral area should be so constructed that, by the removal of the flooring of this area in small sections, a pit is revealed which may be used either for dramatic purposes, or to provide accommodation for a large orchestra should it be required for some special musical presentation.

This area of flooring could be designed as a mechanically operated lift to rise and fall as required. Its use as a fore-stage or pit, however, would probably be limited to, at most, one or two productions each year, and the expense involved would hardly be justified. The various levels could be built-up more economically from easily handled rostrum units, which would allow greater flexibility in their arrangement, and, when not required in this position, could be used for scenic effects on the stage.

If a pit is constructed it should be of such a depth that actors may enter it from below, unseen by the audience, and some form of balustrade must be provided which can be placed around the audience side of the pit. It would also be as well to consider the provision of a flight of steps, constructed in sections to fill the whole length of the pit, which could be placed, when required, leading straight up from the pit to the level of the stage, so that actors congregating unseen at

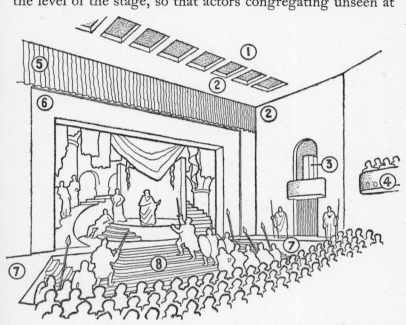

Fig. 20. Diagram illustrating the use of the 'orchestra pit' for dramatic purposes and the use of the side stages

1, grills for built-out fore-stage lighting units. 2, ceiling and walls of auditorium forming 'proscenium opening'. 3, screens covering lighting units and electrician's station in prompt-side stage box. 4, light units in box front. 5, front curtain. 6, adjustable inner proscenium. 7, side stages connecting stage doors to main stage. 8, removable steps set in orchestra pit.

the foot of the steps may make their entry on to the stage either singly or *en masse*. Such steps could be used on the stage proper when not required in front, if they are built-up of easily movable units (see Fig. 20).

For plays where a large fore-stage is needed, the choral area may be built-up to the level of the main stage with rostrum units. It would seem therefore that the front rows of seating may need to be arranged on a flat area of floor, on which the fore-stage may be built, and which could form the choral area, the slope of the auditorium floor starting beyond this area, thereby allowing the fore-stage slightly to overlook the front row of the revised seating. This fore-stage may be anything from 10 to 15 ft. in depth depending on the design of the auditorium. In the case of a Georgian play the fore-stage provided need not be so deep, but, in all these cases, there must be doors in the side walls of the auditorium which will serve the function of the parados in the classic theatre or the stage-doors of the Elizabethan, Restoraton or Georgian theatres. These doors should be placed at the height of the stage proper, with a small landing or side stage joining them to the main stage, and with steps leading down to the floor of the choral area; these steps would be covered over by the fore-stage when it was erected. Off-stage the doors should lead into a small assembly area which will in turn connect with the stage proper through an opening in the proscenium wall.

The provision of a fore-stage in front of the proscenium opening, as outlined above, has one important drawback in that it necessitates the removal of several rows of seating; in a small theatre, such as we are considering here, this is a serious difficulty. Can it be overcome in any way?

The desire for a fore-stage in the contemporary theatre is actuated by the need for the actor to perform within the limits of the auditorium in close contact with his audience, and not, as in the contemporary theatre, behind the proscenium opening in a distinct and separate space. The problem, therefore, is to include within the limits of the auditorium a portion of the stage on which actors may perform, and on which scenery may be placed: it must be remembered that scenery may not be used on the audience side of the proscenium wall, except with the written consent of the local authority, and this has been one of the main disadvantages of the normal contemporary fore-stage built in front of the proscenium wall. If it is not possible to extend the stage into the auditorium, would it not be possible to extend the auditorium to include the stage (see Figs. 21 and 26)?

If the theatre were designed in such a way that there were virtually no proscenium opening, the side walls and ceiling of the auditorium forming the limits of the opening, then a fore-stage may be formed by extending the side walls and

Fig. 21. Diagram illustrating the formation of a fore-stage behind the 'proscenium opening' by an extension of the auditorium walls and ceiling

1. grills for fore-stage lighting units. 2, ceiling and walls of auditorium forming 'proscenium opening'. 3, screens covering lighting units and electrician's station in prompt-side stage box. 4, stage door. 5, light units in box front. 6, space for the movement of fire curtain. 7, removable and adjustable ceiling extension piece. 8, removable and adjustable wall extension piece. 9, side stages. 10, front curtain at rear of fore-stage area. 11, fore-stage. 12, footlights.

ceiling of the auditorium to enclose a portion of the main stage.[1] The provision of temporary structures, which may be placed in position on and above the stage when the illusion of a fore-stage is required, would make this possible; these must be arranged so as to allow the safety curtain to descend

[1] For the basis of this theory I am indebted to Mr. Richard Southern. Readers wishing to pursue the subject further may do so in *The Essentials of Stage Planning*. See also: Teaching note 24, Part I, *The History of the English Theatre* by Richard Southern, a film strip by Common Ground Ltd.

in a normal manner cutting the stage off from the audience. The remainder of the stage would now form the rear stage, and the front curtain, if one were required, would be provided at the rear of the fore-stage area. By these means we shall have achieved a fore-stage on which scenery may freely be used, without the loss of a single seat from the auditorium; it will also be found that the problem of sight-lines from the circle or boxes has been greatly eased, as, instead of attempting to provide adequate sight-lines to the main stage area and to a fore-stage area in front of this, the problem is reduced to the provision of adequate sight-lines to the main stage area only. If local regulations permit a choral area may be provided in the same manner by the removal of the front portion of the main stage; the orchestra pit, when required, may also be formed here, covered over by the front of the main stage and open to the audience only on the side nearest to them, thereby providing for an orchestra without creating an actor-audience barrier.

As it is extremely likely that the play of the future will make far greater use of a fore-stage, set in close contact with the audience, than do the plays of the present, the design of the civic theatre should make every allowance for this probability. If the suggestions outlined directly above are to be carried out then the main stage should be designed with a minimum depth from proscenium wall to rear wall of 60 ft., to allow for the provision of a fore-stage of from 10 to 15 ft. in depth; in this case it may be necessary to provide a further entrance to the truck bay in addition to, and directly upstage of, that already described (see Fig. 26) as this will be, to some extent, covered by the O.P. wall extension. As both these openings would not be in use at the same time, it will be possible to make scene packs against the shutter-door of the unused opening. The question of the proscenium opening will be considered in greater detail in the following section.

(a) THE PROSCENIUM OPENING

Consideration must now be given to the main element in this vital link, the proscenium opening. For the box-set type of play, where the working areas of the stage must be concealed from the audience, the proscenium wall, used as a masking element, is a necessary feature, but there may come a time when concealment of the working areas is no longer required. How can this factor be allowed for?

Most local authorities will require that: ' . . . the stage should be separated from the auditorium by a brick proscenium wall . . . the wall shall be carried up to a height of at least 3 ft. above the roof . . . and shall be carried down to a solid foundation. In no part shall the wall be less than 13 in. thick.' The extracts from the L.C.C. rules quoted here continue by stating that: 'no more than three openings, exclusive of the proscenium opening, shall be formed in the proscenium wall', and then state the maximum allowable sizes for these openings. The rules do not, however, lay down either maximum or minimum sizes for the proscenium opening itself, but as the opening must be provided with 'a fire-resisting screen or safety curtain to be used as a drop curtain, of such pattern, construction and gearing, and with such arrangements as may be approved by the Council for pouring water upon the surface of the screen which is towards the stage', its size will be governed by the maximum workable size for such a curtain.[2]

When considering the size of the acting area it was decided that 30 ft. was an average width for a contemporary theatre setting, and when considering the width of the proscenium opening it will be advisable to allow for this size, which will then easily accommodate any touring play that may visit the theatre. The more the size of theatres can be standardized, the easier will be the work of the designer who must design settings for tours. While 30 ft. is the normal width of a set, it will be necessary, from time to time, to stage a production,

[1] See *Home Office Manual*, 1934, sections 59–65, 70.

such as some form of ballet or pageant, which could well do with a wider opening, and so it is as well to build the actual structural opening allowed in the proscenium wall as large as is ever likely to be needed: it being a reasonably simple job to mask this opening down to the required size, whereas, once built too small, no alterations can afterwards be made except at great expense. The play of the future may well demand the larger size, and where immovable structural features are introduced into the design of the theatre they should be conceived in such a way that the maximum altera-

Fig. 22. Diagram illustrating the 'non-existent' proscenium opening, the use of the stage box and the use of a built-out fore-stage replacing several rows of seating

Note: No attempt has been made in Figs. 19, 20, 21, 22, 24 and 25 to suggest any decorative treatment of the auditorium

1, grills for built-out fore-stage lighting units. 2, ceiling and walls of auditorium forming 'proscenium opening'. 3, lighting units in box-front. 4, projected scenery on cyclorama. 5, fore-stage. 6, stage box. 7, stage door.

tions can be made to the building with the minimum possible effort.

The larger width of proscenium opening suggested above should not exceed 40 ft., and the exact height will need to be studied in relation to the sight-lines from the rear of the auditorium, and also from the point of view of providing an opening of pleasant proportions. It should be noted that the width of the acting area will also be correspondingly widened when the larger width of proscenium opening is used, and the stage dimensions must be adjusted accordingly (see Section 8, page 49). So that the proscenium opening may appear to be non-existent, there should be no frame around it, as this will only serve to accentuate the effect of cutting the actor off from the audience. The walls and ceiling of the auditorium should form the limits of the opening. This latter point will decide the height of the opening, which should be as high as is ever likely to be needed. The lines of the walls and ceiling may then, if so required, be continued around the stage area by the use of a cyclorama (see Fig. 22), or may be extended to produce the illusion of a fore-stage set in the auditorium (see Fig. 21).

This large opening, equipped with its fire curtain, should satisfy the needs of the local authority, and a flexible form of inner proscenium may be provided up-stage of this to suit the masking requirements of the 30 ft. wide setting. The inner proscenium should be designed so that it may be quickly and easily altered in the size of its opening to suit any particular setting, and, moreover, so that it may be completely removed when necessary. It will take the place of the tormentor wings found in the contemporary theatre, usually formed of neutral flats or curtains (see Fig. 9), and the box-set may be built right up to it. It is suggested that it may well be possible to incorporate the lighting bridge, mentioned previously, as part of the structure of the inner proscenium, which should be built of some light-weight fire-resisting material. In this case the soffit of this inner proscenium would need to be approximately 1 ft. to 1 ft. 6 in. below the ceiling of any setting used on the stage, so as to allow the spotlights fixed to the bridge to throw their light to the rear of a set. The height of the average setting is from 16 to 18 ft.

This secondary opening should be as plain as possible in its surround, and should be finished with a matt surface so as not to reflect lighting, or to distract the eye of the spectator from the stage. Once again the design should be such that it imposes no feeling of separation between the actor and the audience.

(b) THE STAGE BOX

A further feature of the auditorium which must be discussed under this heading of the connecting link is the stage

box (see Figs. 19, 20, 21, 22, and 23); a traditional feature of the British theatre, its use by actors and also by audience has now almost completely vanished. From an acoustic point of view the breaking-up of the surface of the side walls of the auditorium nearest the proscenium opening by means of boxes, or openings cut into the walls, gives excellent results, and, if only for this reason, it would be worth considering their re-introduction on the lines of the traditional stage

Fig. 23. Diagram illustrating the traditional use of the stage box in a small provincial theatre

doors and box. They could then be used by the actors in the revival of any play in which they were originally used, but care would have to be taken to ensure that they were within the view of the entire audience. This might be arranged by introducing a slight splay into the side walls of the auditorium. It should be remembered that their primary function in the traditional theatre was to provide an additional acting area at a higher level than the stage, but at the same time sufficiently associated with the stage area to enable intimate scenes to be acted as between one player on the stage and another at an upper window or balcony. This end must be kept in view when re-introducing the boxes into the modern theatre, and their height above the stage proper should be so arranged as to permit of such performances (see Fig. 23).

When not required by the cast one of the boxes might well provide a new position where the musicians, displaced from the orchestra pit, could perform their interval, or other, music. The other box might provide a useful position for the electrician, allowing him an excellent view of the acting area of the stage, but screened from the audience by movable screens or curtains. In addition, both boxes would provide useful positions for front-of-house stage lighting units.

11. *The Auditorium*

So THAT THE architect may properly understand the feeling of intimacy which is necessary between the members of the audience and the actors, it would be as well for him to study the designs of some of the smaller provincial theatres of the Georgian, late-Georgian and Regency periods,[1] which managed to strike exactly the right note in intimacy and theatrical feeling. Too often the modern theatre auditorium, designed on scientific lines, has the atmosphere of a sterilized lecture hall rather than that of a theatre. It is most important that the auditorium should suggest in every feature of its design a feeling of pleasure, warmth and theatricality. The old-fashioned horse-shoe auditorium, while it did not provide all the functions required by a modern audience who come both to see and hear the play, at least provided the right feeling amongst the audience, who made a visit to the theatre a social occasion, and were able to see plenty of each other, and of each other's clothes, during the intermissions. The rectangular blocks of seating usually found today do not allow for this social effect, and the shelf-like layers of circles and galleries, piled one above the other (see Fig. 6), split the audience up into a number of separate units each unaware of the other. It is not suggested that the sight-lines should be sacrificed to achieve this intimacy, but it is as well to recall the excellent effects which were achieved by this arrangement in the past and some effort should be made to re-introduce this feeling.

To help in providing the right theatre atmosphere the seating capacity of the auditorium should be limited to a maximum of 700 persons. It is a great deal better to have a small theatre constantly full, than to provide a large building which may be only two-thirds full for the greater part of the

[1] See *The Georgian Playhouse*, Richard Southern, Pleiades, 1948.

time. A full-house has an excellent effect on any theatre company, a half-empty house can have disastrous results. In the average sized provincial town, with each play running for sixteen or twenty-four performances, a theatre of this capacity will readily seat the available audience; if a play is an overwhelming success, and it is not possible to accommodate all who wish to see it in the run usually allotted, the play can always be continued for a further period. It is assumed that a civic theatre of the kind under discussion will be exempt from paying entertainment tax, as otherwise it might be necessary to increase the seating capacity, so that the price of seats could be kept within the means of the average member of the community, but the promoters should strive for the best theatre conditions possible within the limits of sound economics.

A difficulty presents itself at this stage however, in that an auditorium seating only 700, while providing for the financial maintenance of a permanent repertory company, could not take sufficient money in one week to pay the costs of a visiting ballet company. It would need an auditorium of double the size, seating at least 1500 persons, to cover such an expense. This difficulty might be overcome by providing a theatre to seat the larger number, which could be reduced by mechanical means to provide the smaller auditorium required for dramatic purposes,[2] but it would probably be far wiser to play such limited seasons of ballet at a loss in the smaller theatre. Some towns may find it hard to afford the initial expense of an additional hall for orchestral concerts, but this should be provided in addition to the theatre wherever possible. While the available theatre audience can be spaced out over a week or a fortnight, the visiting orchestra will seldom be able to play more than one or two nights, and therefore the available audience will need to be accommodated in this short period, and it follows that the concert hall will need to accommodate a far larger number of persons than

[2] *The Civic Theatre, Malmo, Sweden*, Architectural Review, March, 1946. Building, January 1947. Architect and Building News, 20 April 1945.

the theatre. While the use of the theatre both for concerts and drama might seem to provide a logical solution in cases of straightened finance, it must be borne in mind that the routine of theatre performances proper would be seriously upset if concerts were given on any other days than Sundays; moreover the architect would find himself involved in complications arising from the attempt to provide ideal acoustics for both dramatic speech and orchestral concerts in one and the same building. While on the subject of multi-purpose buildings, it might be worth while to study the practicability of designing a portion of the sloping floor of the auditorium in such a way that it could be raised to a flat position,[3] thus providing for the occasional use of the theatre for civic balls, but, in relation to the primary function of the building, this would be open to the same objection as that noted above if the special uses were demanded too frequently, and the expense of equipping the theatre in this way for occasional use only would probably not be easy to justify. If the promoters intend to provide for a permanent professional theatre company, they would be well advised to concentrate on providing a building which is ideally suited to the requirements of an acting company and is always available for their use: the need for a separate hall for concerts and other social purposes would therefore seem to be an inevitable conclusion.

(a) THE SHAPE OF THE AUDITORIUM

The shape of the auditorium will be limited by two main factors:

1. That every member of the audience shall be able to see the whole of the acting area.
2. That every member of the audience shall be close enough to the actors to experience the necessary feeling of intimacy.

Having eliminated the orchestra pit it should now be possible to place the front row of seats between 6 and 10 ft.

[3] See *The Corso Theatre, Zurich*, Architectural Review, December 1938, September 1946. See also: *The Essentials of Stage Planning.*

from the front edge of the stage. The overall width of the seating should not be greater than 30 ft., the width of the average proscenium opening (see Fig. 15), and, ideally, this width should be maintained to the rear of the auditorium. However, so that the persons seated at the rear of the theatre may still be placed as near to the stage as possible, a compromise must be made and the seating fanned out very slightly to give more space for seats nearer the stage; but this tendency should be severely limited. The provision of parallel side walls, unless well broken by openings or recesses, is likely to prove a decided disadvantage when the acoustics are being considered, and the slight fan-shape will therefore prove advantageous from this point of view also. It must, however, be strongly stressed that the fan-shaped auditorium when carried to extremes does not allow for good sight-lines to the stage, and its use should therefore be treated with the greatest of care.[4] It has already been suggested that the seating should be arranged on a slight curve, and this would help to provide good sight-lines.

The main point that must always be borne in mind by the theatre architect is that every person who has paid for a seat is entitled to see the entire play, and so even the people seated on the extremities of the rows should be able to see the entire acting area. There is nothing more exasperating for a scenic designer than having to design sets for a theatre which has bad sight-lines, or for a member of the audience who, through no fault of the scenic designer, is unable to see the whole of the setting and is condemned to follow much of the play by sound alone.

The London County Council state in their requirements that no seat, whose dimensions conform to their minimum requirements—2 ft. 6 in. back to back and 1 ft. 8 in. arm to arm —shall be placed at a greater distance than 10 ft. from a gangway leading to an exit. This distance may, however, be in-

---

[4] See *Theatre acoustics: some results and warnings*, by H. Bagenal, R.I.B.A Journal 1939, Vol. xlvi, p. 500. *Planning for good acoustics*, by Bagenal and Wood, Methuen 1931. *Practical acoustics*, by H. Bagenal, Methuen 1942.

creased, with the consent of the local authority, where their measurements for the seating are exceeded. In the design of the seating it would be as well to apportion the least useful part of the auditorium to the gangways, and these are obviously the areas down the side walls. This arrangement makes the provision of a central gangway necessary if the utmost use is to be made of the available space. A central gangway, however, tends to give an impression of emptiness to the actor, and so the front rows of seating should be arranged to carry right across the auditorium in an unbroken curve. The distance back-to-back of these seats will have to be increased to provide what are virtually gangways between each row of seats.[5] Behind these seats we may introduce such gangways as would naturally conform with the regulations. If the theatre is designed on an open site, with more than adequate fire exits, the local authority may be amenable to relaxing some of their more stringent requirements.

(b) BOXES, CIRCLE OR GALLERY

So that the depth of the auditorium should not be too great, it may be necessary to introduce a circle or gallery, with an allocation of seats of, say, 500 downstairs and 200 upstairs. Sight-lines from the circle must be closely watched to ensure that full vertical visibility is maintained from all seats, not only of the actor on stage level but also of an actor playing on a raised balcony, with headroom under, at the rear of the acting area. In this respect it will be necessary to watch the seats at the rear of the ground floor, vertical vision from which may be impeded by the soffit of the circle. The introduction of a circle, however, while allowing a greater number of the audience to be placed nearer to the stage than would be possible without its use, raises two problems which we have already mentioned: first, it divides the audience into two distinctly separate sections, each totally cut off from the

---

[5] See *Home Office Manual*, 1934, sections 23–24. If the front rows of seating are limited to a length of 30 ft. as outlined above, then this arrangement will conform with the Home Office suggestions.

other, and second, it cuts off the section of audience seated
in the circle from any reasonably direct contact with the actor
on the stage. It will doubtless be conceded that, while the
persons seated at the rear of the ground floor block of seats
are still in contact with the actor through the medium of the
group itself (assuming, or course, that the theatre is full),
the persons at the front of the group being in direct contact
with the actor, those seated in the circle have no contact
either with this group or with the stage. In the tradidional
theatre this problem was overcome by the provision of side
boxes set in the walls and arranged at the same levels as the
circles and gallery, but this system only worked perfectly
when the actor was on a stage set in the auditorium. The need
for good sight-lines to an enclosed stage being now recognized
as of paramount importance, this arrangement can no longer
be used. How then can we relate these two problems of good
sight-lines and of audience-actor contact?

The use of a horseshoe-shaped circle would seem at first
sight to be an obvious solution, providing both adequate
seating within the prescribed horizontal sight-lines and allowing the two separate audience units to be aware of each
other, at the same time bringing a portion of the circle group
within reach of the actor. Unfortunately, where the use of a
built-out fore-stage or
sunken pit is to be con-
sidered, this arrange-
ment of the circle
creates too many diffi-
culties in the vertical
sight-lines to be practi-
cal and some other solu-
tion must be sought:
for example, it might
be a satisfactory ar-
rangement to provide
a normal circle or bal-
cony in contact with

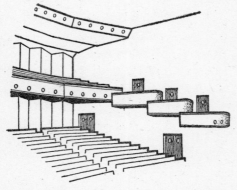

Fig. 24. Diagram of auditorium illustrating
the use of a small circle connected to the stage
by side boxes

F

the actor and the audience below by means of a series of
boxes stepped down along the side walls of the auditorium,
and projecting a sufficient distance from the walls to bring
the persons seated therein within the necessary horizontal
sight-lines of the auditorium (see Fig. 24). These boxes could
be reached, either from a stepped gangway leading up the
side of the auditorium against the walls, or from a corridor
outside. The former arrangement will probably be found the
most desirable when the question of fire escapes from the
auditorium direct to the open air comes under consideration.

The re-introduction of some form of box seating, with
good visibility to the stage, would probably be very popular
with members of the audience who like to visit the theatre in
parties or in family groups; this arrangement would enable
them to enjoy the play as a social unit and not as a long
spaced-out line as is usually the case today. Indeed, this
feature might be taken further, and in place of a deep circle
or balcony, the rear wall of the auditorium might be occupied
by three levels of narrow boxes arranged one above the other,
the upper two tiers of which would together seat the number
of persons otherwise placed in the circle. The lower boxes

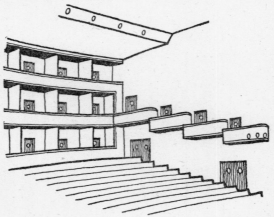

Fig. 25. Diagram of auditorium illustrating the arrangement of boxes across the rear wall, connected to the
stage by side boxes

would accommodate the persons who would otherwise be seated in the rear rows of the ground floor seats, thus bringing the apparent rear wall of the auditorium nearer to the stage (see Fig. 25). If these boxes were planned with a maximum depth of 9 ft., the persons seated in them would in no way be cut off from the remainder of the audience. The provision of vertical supports or screens between the boxes, if required, could be arranged in such a way that they would not interfere with any sight-lines. The upper boxes would still be connected with the stage by side boxes in the manner set out previously. This treatment of the rear wall will be seen to be an added advantage when the acoustics of the theatre are being considered.

(c) DECORATION AND COMFORT

In general the tendency in the new theatre should be to equal the comfortable conditions provided in the modern cinema. If the theatre is being built on an open site then it should be possible to allow plenty of room for seating, and really adequate allowance must be made for leg-room. While comfort is most desirable, any tendency on the part of the audience to lounge should be held in check, and the design of the seats should be such that the audience are encouraged to sit up and take notice of the play.

Adequate heating and ventilation must be provided not only in the auditorium but also in the entire theatre, heating being particularly important on the stage.[6] The gaiety and gala feeling of the auditorium decoration should be supplemented by the colourful use of lighting. As to decoration, many people immediately associate the word 'theatre' with a visual impression of a pleasing array of gilt, cream, red plush and cupids. Is it possible to design a contemporary decoration which will create as good an atmosphere as did

[6] See *Air Conditioning* by J. A. Moyer and Raymond U. Fittz, McGraw-Hill Book Co. Inc., 1938, chapters XIII, XIV. *Air Conditioning for Comfort* by Samuel R. Lewis, Keeney Publishing Co. Inc., 1938, chapter 16. *Principles of Heating and Ventilation* by Oscar Faber and J. R. Kell, The Architectural Press, 1945, chapter XIX.

those decorations of the theatres of the last century? Whatever decoration is provided the primary aim of the designers
should be to further the required feeling of intimacy: large
areas of plain plastered wall surface should be avoided, especially in those areas separating the proscenium opening from
the audience seated in any circle or upper boxes, as these
plain wall surfaces tend to act as vast cycloramas, and give a
feeling of space and distance disproportionate to the areas
which they actually occupy.

(d) LIGHTING

This subject is dealt with here only in so far as it will affect
the architect in his designs; it is the one subject of theatre
design which has been reasonably fully written up, and much
information is available. The architect would be well advised,
however, to consult a qualified stage lighting expert at a very
early stage in the designs.[7]

The architect should allow space in the design of the
auditorium for a number of lighting units which will be used
mainly in relation to the stage. If provision is to be made for
a 'built-out fore-stage' then a number of 'acting-area' lanterns
should be arranged above the ceiling of the auditorium in
positions where they may project light directly down on to
the built-out fore-stage. The source of light should not, of
course, be visible to the audience, and may well be arranged
above a series of open coffers designed in the ceiling; these
coffers will also be found to be invaluable when considering
the acoustic design (see Figs. 19, 20, 21, and 22).[8]

Mention has already been made of the stage-boxes as
possible positions for stage lighting, and spotlights may be
built into the fronts of the circle or side boxes. Such lighting

[7] See *Stage Lighting, Principles and Practice* by Ridge and Aldred'
Pitmen, 1940. *Stage Lighting*, Ridge, Cambridge, 1935. *A Method of
Lighting the Stage* by McCandless, Theatre Arts, Inc., 1939. *Stage Lighting
for Amateurs'* by P. Goffin, Frederick Muller, 1938. *The Technique of
Stage Lighting* by R. G. Williams, Pitmans. *Tabs*, a free journal obtain-
able from Strand Electric, Ltd. *Home Office Manual*, 1934, sections 86–101.
[8] See example: *Shakespeare Memorial Theatre, Stratford-on-Avon.*

units must be readily accessible for maintenance and cleaning, and also for pre-setting their 'throw' and focus for any particular play. Unless they can be reached by a person situated out of sight of the audience they will not be moved during the performance of a play, and any necessary changes of colour must be carried out by the use of specially fitted lighting units, which are remotely controlled at the main switch-board.

A cove arranged in the ceiling of the auditorium, some two-thirds of the distance from the proscenium wall to the rear wall, could conceal further stage lighting for use either with the fore-stage or on the main stage (see Figs. 24 and 25). Cat-walks above the ceiling should be arranged to provide access to all these points so that the throw of lights may be altered even during the performance of a play. The positions of the lights, and the access to them, should be arranged to allow the technician adjusting them a good view of the stage below, whilst himself being hidden from the view of the audience.

While on the subject of auditorium lighting some mention should be made of the possibility for including a projection room in the design. This should be built high up in the rear wall of the auditorium, or in the ceiling at the rear of the auditorium, as the design permits. It might be used, at times, for stage lighting effects, and would also provide a useful position from which the electrician could control, by means of a secondary switch-board, any intricate arrangements of stage lighting which required direct vision of the stage for accurate cueing. The inclusion of a loud-speaker system relaying sound from the stage to this room—and incidentally to the dressing rooms, green-room and similar areas of the theatre—would greatly facilitate such control by the electrician, or even by the stage director who could also use this vantage point, in addition to or in place of his prompt corner control station, for a complete control of all stage operations by means of cue lights and telephonic communication. In this case the room must be so designed that there is no possibility of any sound within being heard by the adjoining audience. The inclusion of such a room would allow the theatre to be used on Sundays for performances by the local Film Society: in this case of course the necessary restrictions governing the planning of projection rooms must be followed.

On the stage itself, provision must be made for a number of lighting points into which may be plugged the leads or cables of the lights used on the stage. These points are usually arranged below the level of the stage, and are reached through small metal trap doors or 'dips' (see Figs, 9 and 12). Three or four dips should be spaced out on either side of the acting area, and a further three dips arranged across the stage in front of the position where the cyclorama will stand. In addition to these, plug points should be spaced out along the on-stage edge of the fly-gallery into which the cables from any overhead lighting may be plugged, and further points should be located on the grid itself.

When the design of the inner proscenium is being considered, it should be made possible for spots or vertical lighting strips to be fixed to the up-stage side of this unit in such a way that their light may be directed into the set. Mention of footlights has already been made in section 7 (a).

Under the heading of lighting in general, the size and position of the room necessary to accommodate the electrician's switch-board must be considered; this will control both the stage and the front-of-house lighting. In addition to any use which the electrician may make of the projection room mentioned above, space for the installation of the switch-board proper should be allocated in or near the prompt corner of the stage. It has already been suggested that the stage box on this side of the stage might be used for this purpose, and an area at the rear of this box, and at the same level, connecting through an opening in the proscenium wall with the stage proper should be provided. The opening should give access to a light platform some 2 ft. 6 in. wide overlooking the stage area, and allowing the electrician good visibility of both acting area and the stage generally; it could quite easily form the roof of the stage director's control station. There should be easy access for the electrician from his room to stage level, and this may be in the form either of a spiral stair or of a vertical cat ladder. It would also be convenient if access to the lighting stations over the auditorium and to the projection room were made as easy as possible from the electrician's room.

The switch-board, for which accommodation must be allowed, may be anything up to 12 ft. long by 2 ft. deep, with a minimum depth of 2 ft. behind and 3 ft. in front for access. A height of 7 ft. will allow space above the board for conduit connections. The board must be so arranged that the electrician may have access to the rear of the board for maintenance, as well as to the front. The electrician's room should be in telephonic and light communication with the stage director's control station, as in fact will be all the working areas of the stage, flies, etc. An electrical intake room should be planned under this area in the basement of the theatre.

12. *Workshops and Storerooms*

BEFORE CONSIDERING IN detail the planning of this section, the different uses to which the theatre may be put must be reviewed, since these will have a direct bearing on the design of this area of the building. It has already been stated that a civic theatre may be run in two different ways; it may present what has been called a repertory season in which a different play is produced every two or three weeks, or it may run its season on a repertoire basis, when some two or three different plays will be performed each week. In addition to its primary function of providing drama for its own theatre audience, the building may well form the central unit for the provision of drama for the whole county, and the workshops and scene stores will then need to cater not only for the theatre productions but also for the smaller touring productions which will be sent around the village halls. If the theatre is to be run on repertory lines the workshops and storage space will not be overlarge. The latter will only be required to store the stock scenery from which the different productions are built up, and while the scenery for the present production is standing on the stage the workshops will be dealing with the scenery for the following production. What then is the difference if a repertoire season is to be performed? As several plays are performed each week, and may be repeated at intervals throughout the season, it follows that the scenery for these productions must be kept available for use at any time. This implies that not only will the theatre need to carry a far larger stock of scenery, but it will also need much larger storage space where the completed settings may be stored. It must be remembered that it is not always possible to 'break-down' a set into all its various units, as some settings may need large built-up units of steps, rostrums, etc., which it must be possible to store complete. Because of these problems it is most probable that the more usual repertory system will be employed in the theatre, especially as the present-day repertory theatres have built up an audience used to a weekly or fortnightly change of programme. These are, however, points on which the architect and the theatre promoters should decide at an early stage in the designing of the building, and if it is decided to cover both a county touring scheme and also a drama school, then the workshops and scene stores must be enlarged accordingly.

(*a*) THE WORKSHOP

The workshop considered here is for a theatre run on repertory lines. When a new play is to be produced every two or three weeks the scenery must be prepared in the

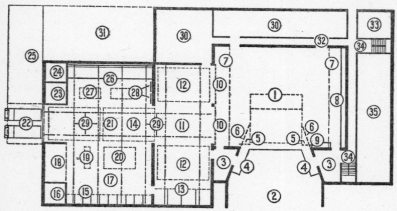

Fig. 26. Diagrammatic plan of stage and surrounding workshops, storage areas, offices, etc.

1, the stage. 2, auditorium. 3, assembly areas. 4, stage doors and side stages. 5, adjustable inner proscenium. 6, auditorium wall extension pieces to form fore-stage. 7, fly-galleries over. 8, single-purchase counter-weight system enclosed behind light partition wall, with access panels, the system worked from the fly-gallery. 9, stage director's control station. 10, fire-resisting shutter doors. 11, truck bay. 12, truck. 13, storage bays for trucks and rostrums. 14, workshop. 15, storage bays for flats with storage space for backcloths over. 16, master carpenter's room. 17, backcloth assembly area. 18, timber store. 19, carpenter's bench. 20, flat canvassing bench. 21, workshop assembly area. 22, covered loading dock. 23, artist's office. 24, paint store. 25, wash-down area. 26, paint-frame and gallery. 27, painting area. 28, scene packs for current use on paint-frame. 29, overhead pulley tracks. 30, furniture, property and electrician's stores. 31, future extension to stores. 32, passage way and double doors. 33, doorkeeper's office, etc. 34, stairs to dressing rooms and basement. 35, area for green-room, office dressing rooms, lavatories, etc.

theatre building, and it is usual in repertory theatres to employ a carpenter and scenic artist and their assistants for this purpose; in this respect this form of theatre will be seen to vary from the normal London commercial theatre, where all the scenery is prepared in advance by outside firms. Although a large stock of scenery in the form of standard size flats will be kept in the theatre, it will nevertheless be necessary, from time to time, to build specially shaped flats, and also to repair, re-canvas and generally keep in good order such flats as are available. A special shop is required for this purpose, and also for the assembly of the flats required to build a set in advance on one of the trucks.

It has already been suggested that the workshop area should communicate directly with the truck bay, and the shop should be planned in such a manner that the most direct approach possible to the stage should be achieved.

The actions which should be considered when planning the workshop area are as follows:[1] A certain amount of timber, in the form of battens or plywood sheets, will, from time to time, be brought into the theatre and will be stored ready for later use. If a county drama scheme is envisaged the scenery for the village tours will be brought back to the theatre at the end of a tour, unloaded at the loading dock and run to the scene stores. If, on the other hand, an outside touring play is to perform in the civic theatre it should be possible to unload the scenery from the lorries, and then run it straight through to its position on the stage in one straightforward simple movement.

When a new production is being prepared for use in the theatre, the designer (artist) and the carpenter will pick out from the scene store the flats which they intend to use. If any of these require altering in any way they will be packed in an area adjacent to the carpenter's work benches, the remainder

[1] See *Scenery for the Theatre* by H. Burris Meyer and E. D. Cole, Harrap 1939. Although this book deals primarily with American practice and procedure, it will afford an invaluable guide to general back-stage methods and requirements. *Behind the Scenes at a Theatre* by Richard Southern, Common Ground Film strip, CGB 202.

will be run to bays or packs located near the painting area. When alterations and painting are complete the scenery will either be assembled to form a setting on a truck in the workshop assembly area, or will be run straight through to the stage. In the case of small, awkwardly shaped settings built on trucks, it is often advisable to assemble the setting on the truck first, and then the artist will paint the set as an entire unit. This procedure should be allowed for in the design of the assembly and painting areas.

When scenery is painted ready for use on the village tour it will be packed near the loading dock ready for removal by lorry. On the completion of a production in the theatre the scenery is either run directly from the stage in single units and returned to the scene stores, or if a truck is being used, the scenery is dismantled in the workshop assembly area and returned to the store.

Theatre scenery is painted with water paint, and the artist will commence work by painting out the old design on a flat and then proceed to superimpose the new design on the priming coat. After this action has been repeated a number of times the flats will become thick with several layers of paint, and they should then be washed and scraped clean; for this purpose an area outside the building should be set aside for use as a wash-down space, and this should be of sufficient size to accommodate the largest backcloth, and a supply of water should be made available. The canvas will only stand a certain amount of cleaning, and it must then be removed and the timber frame of the flat must be re-canvassed. This re-canvassing, repairing and alteration of flats to suit the requirements of a particular play will be the chief duties of the carpenter, who will also be responsible for the maintenance of the stage area.

In addition to the larger scenic requirements mentioned, the workshop area must also be used for the construction of special pieces of furniture, fire-places, etc., and for the making, maintaining and repairing of rostrums, steps and other such pieces of scenery required in the theatre.

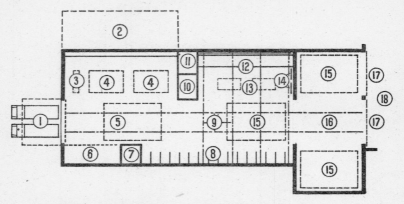

Fig. 27. Diagrammatic plan of workshop and painting area for a combined repertory theatre and county drama scheme headquarters

See also the arrangement of the workshop areas at Malmo, Sweden, footnote on page 77. Here the workshops are placed on the prompt side of the stage; a workable arrangement, but one which is liable to cause an accumulation of traffic in the region of the prompt corner control station. It may, however, be argued that this arrangement allows the stage director greater control over the movement of scenery.

Note: In designs where it is not possible to include a truck bay, the workshop area should connect directly with the stage.

1, covered loading dock. 2, wash-down area. 3, carpenter's bench. 4, flat canvassing benches. 5, workshop assembly area. 6, timber store. 7, master carpenter's room. 8, storage bays for flats, trucks and rostrums, with storage area for backcloths over. 9, pulley tracks over. 10, paint store. 11, artist's office. 12, paint-frame and gallery. 13, painting area for work on flats laid horizontally. 14, scene packs for current use on paint-frame. 15, truck. 16, truck bay. 17, fire-resisting shutter doors. 18, stage.

To provide for all these requirements the workshop should be planned on a generous scale. For the purpose of building or re-canvassing flats, the carpenter will require space for at least one working bench or trestle; if village touring shows are to be catered for in the workshop in addition to the normal theatre productions, then space for at least two such benches must be allowed. Each bench must be capable of holding a single 18 ft. by 6 ft. flat, but provision should be made for the occasional construction of a flat 8 ft. wide, or for the hinging together of two 6 ft. wide flats to form one 12 ft. wide 'book' flat. This latter operation would require an area of 18 ft. by 12 ft. The benches or trestles would best be designed in such a way that they might be folded up and removed to leave a free floor space. In addition there must be at least one normal sized carpenter's bench, 9 to 11 ft. long by 2 ft. 9 in. wide, for the construction of the smaller items of scenery. A space where a new backcloth may be assembled should also be included, and should be at least 6 ft. wide and the length of the longest cloth. Here the canvas will be attached at top and bottom to the timber battens which extend the full width of the backcloth.

While the amount of new construction work carried out in the workshop would scarcely warrant the introduction of power-driven machinery on a large scale, it would be advisable to provide a number of power points around the area of the shop to enable electric screw-drivers, etc., to be used if they can be provided. The installation of a mechanically-operated jig-saw would be an invaluable help when profiles are being cut from plywood or hard-board.

The workshop assembly area should be planned to allow for the possible erection of a complete setting on a 30 ft. by 20 ft. truck: an ideal arrangement would be to provide an area the full size of the acting area of the stage, but this is not essential. The assembly area should be planned in close proximity to the painting area, and it should be possible to run a truck straight from the assembly area through the truck bay and on to the stage in one simple and easy movement.

The whole workshop area must have really good natural and artificial lighting, the former preferably in the form of north-light roof trusses, and it should be high enough to take the tallest scenery required in the theatre. In addition there must be a small flying height above the scenery to facilitate the assembly of scenery to form the required settings; a clear height of shop of 30 ft. should prove ample. The provision of tracks, at some 15 ft. centres, across the workshop at the highest level, with movable pulley blocks running on each track, each with its own separate hauling wire or line, would provide a means of raising and manœuvring ceilings and heavy pieces of scenery into position (see Figs. 26, 27 and 28).

(b) SCENE PAINTING

Having provided for the building and reconditioning of the scenery, consideration must be given to the second part in the preparation of scenery for use on the stage, namely

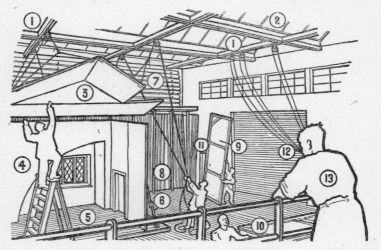

Fig. 28. Diagrammatic view of a workshop from the paint gallery

1, overhead tracks and pulleys. 2, north-light roof trusses. 3, built-up ceiling for scenery. 4, box setting. 5, truck or wagon. 6, extending brace and stage screw. 7, backcloth store. 8, flat store. 9, flat. 10, flat canvassing bench. 11, door to timber store. 12, door to loading dock. 13, artist on paint gallery.

the painting of the flats and backcloths. On the Continent it is usual to paint scenery while it is lying flat on the floor, the painter walking across the scenery to any point he wishes to reach, but, as was seen in the historical section, there was little available space in the traditional British theatre for this extravagant use of floor space, and so the scenery was painted in a vertical position whilst fixed to a movable frame. This frame was normally placed at the rear of the stage, as being the only available position, and was made to rise and fall past the floor of a raised paint-room or gallery situated at the level of the fly-galleries.

At first sight this might appear to be an excellent position for the paint-frame, possessing as it does both adequate flying height for the largest scenery, while at the same time allowing the artist an excellent view of his unfinished work, as he can go into the auditorium and study it from the point of view of the audience. In practice, however, it does not work out quite so well as this, as it is usual in repertory work to leave, if not all, at least part of the current scenery standing on the stage, and this will usually block his view very effectively. An added disadvantage is the difficulty of working on a frame in such a position when the stage is being used for a rehearsal or for a production, for, in addition to the inconvenience of attempting to work without making the slightest noise, the artist may have the added inconvenience of having to put out all his lights whenever a total black-out is required on the stage. The only way to overcome these difficulties is to enclose the paint-room or gallery, but this then defeats any attempt by the artist to stand back and view his work.

It might be argued that if we cannot use the stage side of this wall, then the paint-frame can be placed on the reverse side of the wall. With this arrangement, however, it will be impossible to get a good view of the painting, unless the paint-frame forms part of a large room such as the workshop, set at the rear of the stage, but this is a bad position for the workshop as it is not then possible to arrange for a straight run for the scenery to the stage. Added to this is the difficulty involved in moving a backcloth 30 to 40 ft. long from its position on the stage to the paint-frame. To complete this manœuvre the backcloth must be turned through a half-circle, and this movement takes up a great deal of space, and would involve the striking and resetting of a great deal of scenery every time a cloth had to be moved.

It is obvious that the only really efficient place both for the workshop and the paint-frame is in some position where a backcloth may be lowered from its position in the flies to the stage, be rolled up and then carried *end on* to its required position, without there being any need to circulate the cloth.

We have already planned the workshop in just such a position in its relation to the stage, and therefore the placing of the paint-frame in the workshop would appear to be the most practical solution to the problem. Against this solution it may be argued that the artist should be cut off from the carpenter's shop on account of noise and flying sawdust, but any disadvantage arising from these points is offset by the fact that if the designer is also the painter it will be of great value for him to be placed in a position where he can keep an eye on the work of the carpenter, and can check him at once if he sees that some order has been misunderstood.

If this arrangement is to be carried out, it would be best to extend the width of the workshop so that the painting area may be located against the up-stage wall of the workshop, i.e. the wall which corresponds to the rear wall of the stage. In this position there will be no need for any circulation of the backcloths. The paint-frame will need to accommodate the largest pieces of scenery which are ever likely to be used in the theatre, and as a backcloth may be anything from 40 to 50 ft. wide, according to the sight-lines of the theatre, it follows that the paint-frame will also need to be this length and the workshop must be planned to allow for its inclusion. With the paint-frame located in this position the artist will have a reasonable view of his work across the full width of the shop, and he has the added advantage of being completely cut off from the stage; with the shutter down separating the workshop from the stage, both artist and carpenter may work how and when they like without fear of interrupting rehearsals or productions.

As has been stated earlier, the traditional approach to the design of the paint-frame has been to provide a frame which moved past a fixed floor. This arrangement calls for a clear working height exceeding twice the height of the tallest cloth or other scenery to be painted, an arrangement which worked admirably when the paint-frame was set at the rear of the stage where flying height was already provided. In this case, however, a 60 ft. high workshop would be both excessive

and unnecessary, and unless the required height can be provided by arranging stores under the stage (see Fig.
29), or by building an additional floor
above the workshop, then an alternative arrangement must be sought.

Such an arrangement would be to
provide a paint-gallery which moves
past a fixed frame, in this way only
sufficient height is needed in which to
hang the backcloth, which may be
anything up to 30 ft. deep. This then
might seem to be an ideal arrangement
in the present case, as the workshop
has already been designed with a clear
height of 30 ft., extra height over the
paint-frame can be arranged by the
provision of a north-light truss running the full length of the frame.
The artist's gallery, at least 6 ft.
wide, should be counter-weighted, and
made to rise and fall from floor level
to within head-room height of the
ceiling. A safety rail must be pro-

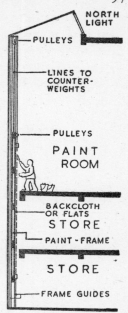

Fig. 29. Section illustrating the use of basement
stores to provide the re-
quired height for the
movement of a paint-
frame past a paint-room

vided on the side farthest from the frame, and access must
be allowed at one end so that flats may be brought into position and set-up on the frame. Backcloths may well be manœu-
vred into position on the frame by means of the movable
pulleys mentioned above, and they will then be stretched on
the frame while the painting is being performed.

It must be remembered, however, that the moving gallery
has definite drawbacks: the difficulty of making satisfactory
connections to a sink or to a gas ring on the gallery limits
the scenic artist to pre-mixing his colours in a room where
these items may more easily be installed, and has the added
disadvantage of causing him to bring his gallery to the level
of the paint-room every time he wishes to fetch some article

which he may have overlooked. Obviously the better arrangement is to provide a paint-room or area where he has everything to hand while carrying out his work, and past which the paint-frame may move, and every endeavour, within the limits imposed by financial and site restrictions, should be made to provide this ideal arrangement.

Fig. 30. Diagrammatic view of a paint gallery and workshop

1, flat canvassing bench. 2, men raising a flat into a vertical position. 3, movable paint gallery. 4, backcloth on paint-frame. 5, pulleys on overhead tracks. 6, north-light roof truss.

One further point concerning the paint-frame should be borne in mind: if the workshops are to cater for a large amount of additional scenery for use on the county tours, or in a separate experimental theatre, then it will be necessary to provide an additional paint-frame. This need not be as large as that already discussed, a length of 30 to 35 ft. being sufficient, as all backcloths can be painted on the larger frame, and only flats be painted on the second frame. It is quite possible, however, that the scenery used for the village tours will be limited to a height of 10 ft., or at the most 12 ft., and in this case the provision of an additional paint-frame would hardly be necessary. Space, however, should be provided where the flats may be painted in a horizontal position either on the floor or on trestles.

(c) LOADING DOCK

The loading dock should be directly accessible to the various storage areas of the workshop, and would best be placed in the wall directly opposite to the entrance to the truck bay so that backcloths may, if necessary, be carried directly from a lorry through the workshop area and on to the stage, end on and with no corners to negotiate. In the same way, if an outside touring play is to be presented in the civic theatre, it should be possible to unload the scenery from the lorries, and then run it straight to its position on the stage in one straightforward simple movement.

If scenery is to be unloaded outside the building, the actual scene doors leading into the building need not be larger than 12 ft. high by 6 ft. wide, as these dimensions are already greater than those of the entrance to a railway scenery truck, and all scenery to be toured will naturally be limited in size by this feature. Flats, whatever their height, although moved in a vertical position inside the theatre, are always dropped on to their sides and carried in a horizontal position when they are being moved from one theatre to another. The height of the doors is therefore determined by the width of the flats, which are in turn limited to a maximum of 8 ft. by the size of the railway truck.

Where space permits it would be as well to provide sliding doors or rolling shutters in the outer wall, of sufficient size to allow for the passage of vehicles into a loading dock situated within the limits of the building (see Fig 31). It is essential that the floor of the loading dock platform be at the same level as the general floor level of the workshop and stage areas, and it is best designed at tail-board height of an average

Fig. 31. Diagram illustrating an internal loading dock

lorry. This factor is one of the main features to be taken into account when the architect is considering his design in section.

Even if there is insufficient space for an internal loading dock, all loading and unloading must be carried out under cover, and with adequate protection from the weather. It must be borne in mind that it may not always be possible to obtain a covered lorry for transporting the scenery, and it should therefore be possible to load an open lorry under cover, which can then be covered with a tarpaulin before being sent out into the rain. Stage scenery, being painted with water paint, can be badly damaged by a little rain.

(*d*) SCENE STORES

These may be divided into three sections: storage space for flats and backcloths, storage space for rostrums and built-up scenery, and stores for the materials from which the scenery is constructed. All these areas should be directly accessible to the workshop area and to the loading dock.

Flats should be stored in a vertical position and for this purpose, bays, some 6 ft. deep by 4 to 5 ft. wide, may be formed along one wall of the workshop by means of metal tubes projecting from the wall (see Figs. 28 and 32). Each flat when stored, is numbered on its outer edge, so that any particular flat may be picked out at will by reference to a catalogue. Space should be allowed for the storage of at least

150 flats for use in the theatre, further space will be required for any additional flats for outside use. The average thickness of flats varies between 1½ and 2 in., and one hundred flats may be stored in these bays in a space approximately 15 ft. long. The space over the bays may be floored in and utilized as storage space for timber or backcloths. In this case the overhead pulley tracks, previously mentioned, must be situated conveniently near to facilitate the raising and lowering of the articles to be stored here. The wall opposite to that

Fig. 32. Diagram illustrating the use of metal
bays for the storage of flats

occupied by the paint-frame may be used for the storage of rolled-up cloths which can be raised to metal shelves projecting from the wall by means of the overhead pulleys. An alternative position can be arranged under the workshop, the cloths being lowered through a long trap cut in the floor and then stored side by side on a series of trestles.

It will probably be found that it is possible to extend the truck bay on either its up- or down-stage side, thereby providing a general storage space where rostrums, trucks and built-up scenery may be stored. A rostrum is usually built so that the top can be lifted off and the legs folded up almost flat, the whole being stored within a width of some 6 to 7 in. Trucks are generally up-ended so that their depth of 3 to 6 in. becomes their width, and they can then be stored, like the flats, in metal bays built out from the wall. Assuming that the trucks are made in standard sizes which can be coupled together as required, then the largest size truck would probably be in the nature of 15 ft. by 10 ft., and it therefore follows that 15 ft. is the height required for their storage. This area should also allow for the storage of such units as will be provided for use as a fore-stage, in addition to any scenery used on the stage itself.

If any height is available over these bays, the top can be floored over and the space used for the storage of such pieces of scenery as are built solidly and cannot be dismantled, i.e., steps, rostrums, etc. To facilitate the movement of such pieces of scenery, further pulley tracks may be installed at ceiling level running up and down the length of the truck bay, and two further tracks may be set at right angles to all those previously mentioned, running through the truck bay and workshop above the space provided for the truck run. These tracks would be at the same level as, and communicating with, the other tracks so that the pulleys may run from one track to another. Vertical ladders should provide access to all these mezzanine floors.

In addition to the areas already mentioned, it is essential to provide a small room for the use of the master carpenter, and space for the safe storage of tools should be arranged here or elsewhere. A store for timber, plywood, glue, canvas and fire-proofing compounds, etc., will also be required. As mentioned at the beginning of the chapter the timber will either be in the form of sheets or in battens in lengths up to 18 or 20 ft. This store should be adjacent both to the loading dock, and to the carpenter's benches. A sink with running water, and two gas rings must be available to the carpenter's work area.

A room for the use of the designer, where he can use a

drawing board and store his models and designs, must be planned near the paint-frame, together with a room for the storage of scene paint and size, where he can mix his colours and keep his brushes. The room should have a large sink with running water, and in addition a tap for filling buckets. There should be two gas rings for heating buckets of water.

(e) FURNITURE, PROPERTY AND ELECTRICIAN'S STORES

The O.P. side of the stage is now occupied by the truck bays, storage spaces for scenery, workshop and paint area. What of the other areas directly adjoining the stage (see Fig. 26)? The area situated at the rear of the stage itself must be considered first. Assuming that the full depth of the stage may at some time be required for acting purposes, it will be necessary to provide a passage-way outside the rear wall, connected to the stage by two double doors. If the site allows, these doors may connect directly across the passage with a series of storerooms running the full width of the stage. These rooms may well be planned as one large area which may be sub-divided at will to form the necessary furniture, electrical and property stores, and property man's and electrician's workshops, all of which must be easily accessible both to the stage and to the workshop area.

The rooms for the electrician need not be large, as most of his equipment always remains in position in the theatre, and the store will be used mainly for the storage of floods and spots on stands, lighting battens in lengths of 6 ft., boxes of bulbs, drawers for the storage of sheets of gelatine and slides, and for such electrical fittings as will be needed from time to time to dress the various settings. Hanging-space for chandeliers and other electrical fittings must be allowed. This store may be divided, if desired, into two sections, one for the heavy equipment and stage dressings in the position already discussed, and the other for light equipment might well be planned in direct connection with the electrician's switch-board, the store being placed at the rear of the switch-board and giving private access to it. The furniture store, on

the other hand, will require an area capable of future expan-
sion, as a permanent repertory company should lay in a stock
of furniture which may be used time and time again, and
will be added to as and when the financial situation permits.
It is always possible to change the appearance of a chair or
sofa by the use of loose covers, and this will mean a great
saving in expenses which would otherwise be incurred by
constantly hiring furniture.

According to Mr Osborne Robinson, the designer to the
Northampton Repertory theatre, the minimum essential basic
furniture stock for a repertory theatre will consist of the
following items, which should all be numbered, catalogued
and stored in separate sections:

A set of Gilt or 'Rococo' furniture: sofas, chairs, tables,
etc.

A set of eighteenth-century 'Chippendale': seats, chairs,
cupboards, desks, bookcases.

A set of early nineteenth-century flavour: couches, pedes-
tals, spinet, stools, tables.

Two sets (at least) of Victorian, for Rich and Lower
Middle class: sideboard, *vis-à-vis*, whatnots, sofas,
tables, chairs, fireplaces, fenders, piano.

A set of Edwardian: sofa, 'nouveau art' chairs, grand
piano, fireplaces, etc.

Two sets of Modern: three-piece suites, desk, radio, bed,
divans, small tables, stools, piano, radiogram.

Historical periods: Tudor, Italian, Medieval: These are
usually faked in the workshop, all very heavy and bulky
to store once made.

A set of Cottage or Rustic furniture.

A set of Garden or Terrace furniture.

A set of Office furniture.

It will readily be seen from the brief list given above that
the space required to store even the minimum amount of
necessary furniture will be large: indeed, the total area of
furniture and property stores together may well correspond

to that of the workshop area. It may therefore be found necessary to allocate to the electrician's and furniture stores the
whole of the area under consideration at stage level, and to
plan the property store to occupy a similar area at a higher
level. The design of the property store suffers from the same
disadvantage as the furniture store, in that the stock of properties will always be growing. Here it should be possible to
store such small items of furnishing, pictures, weapons,
crockery, etc., each in its own section, and space must be
allowed here, or in the furniture stores, for such candelabra
or other hanging fittings as do not come under the control of
the electrician. A section will also be required here, or in the
furniture store, for the storage of built-up fireplace sur-
rounds of different periods and styles; some of these will undoubtedly be very bulky. In addition, there must be racks
for the storage of small carpets and rugs and at least six large
carpets, each capable of covering the floor area of an entire
setting; there must be racks also for the storage of rolled-up
painted stage-cloths of the size of the acting area, unless these
are stored in the scene store with the rolled-up backcloths. It
will be necessary to provide long drawers arranged in tiers
for the storage of artificial flowers, and numerous cupboards
for the storage of china and glass. It would be as well if the
walls of this section were lined with cupboards with sliding
doors. Curtains, tabs, draperies, loose covers and dust covers
may be stored either in this section or with the wardrobe
mistress.

The workroom space allocated to the property man must
provide for the storage of such small properties as are required for the current production. Lock-up cupboard space
is required for the storage of food, cigarettes, etc.; a small
cooker or gas ring, and a sink with hot and cold running water
will also be required to enable the property man and his assistants to prepare and wash-up such simple meals as may be
needed during the action of the play.

It is advisable to plan this group of rooms at stage level so
that food trolleys and other articles required during the action

of the play may be carried direct to the stage as required during the performance. The electrician's room and the furniture store need to be arranged at this level because both involve the movement of heavy objects, and it is obviously desirable to keep such movements as simple and direct as possible.

It may, however, be found that site or financial restrictions limit the use of this area at the rear of the stage, and it may be necessary to provide the required facilities within the compass of the building operations already stipulated for the workshop. In this case it would be as well to arrange the necessary storerooms below the workshop area (see Fig 29), the equality of areas readily allowing for such an arrangement while at the same time making possible the ideal arrangement, already mentioned, for the paint-frame. In this case it will be essential to provide a hoist or lift direct from this area to workshop level, and, in addition, it would be as well to provide a sloping ramp, of easy gradient, connecting the two levels.

Before proceeding to discuss each item in greater detail it is as well to enumerate the other rooms which will need to be readily accessible to the stage. It has already been noted that the main entrance for the actors to the stage itself should be controlled by the stage director's chief assistant the stage manager, and it would be as well if this opening could be designed together with an assembly area of some sort, where crowds or other gatherings of actors could be marshalled under the eye of the stage manager. It must be remembered that, while the actors' entrance to the stage should be in such a position that it can be controlled by the stage manager, the constant flow and movement of persons must not in any way distract the attention of the prompter, or of any person in charge of the control station situated in the prompt corner. The introduction of the assembly area may therefore allow for the necessary control of the entrance, and at the same time divorce it from the region of the control station. So that the assembly area may be readily available to the stage manager it must be planned on the same side of the stage as the control station, i.e. the prompt side, and the rooms provided for the use of the actors, the dressing rooms, green-room, etc., must be directly accessible to it. It is not necessary that the dressing rooms should be planned giving direct access to the stage, nor is it desirable, so long as a green-room is available where the cast may rest without the necessity of returning to their dressing rooms while they are off the stage. The green-room must have adequate lavatory accommodation associated with it, and should be near the stage but not opening directly on to it, as actors and actresses can be very noisy and talkative when not on the stage. A corridor running the length of the side wall of the stage will connect these various rooms with the assembly area, and with the staircases leading up to the dressing rooms and other offices. These should be planned in accordance with any local bye-laws governing their design, and may be built wrapped around the stage block, or in a separate wing.

Three dressing rooms must be planned as near to the stage as possible for use as office-dressing rooms by the producer, the stage director, and the stage manager respectively. In addition a panatrope room, two quick-change rooms and a recess or alcove for the storage of scenery braces, weights and screws will be required in direct contact with the stage, the latter preferably on the O.P. side of the stage.

It should be remembered that actors and actresses may often have to wear voluminous costumes involving them in the management, for example, of such items as panniers or crinolines: all passages, stairs, doorways and lavatories which they are likely to use while in costume, must be planned wide enough to allow free passage-way, and, in particular, there should be no projections from the walls and doors which might catch and tear valuable costumes.

(*a*) GREEN-ROOM

A ROOM FOR the use of the company, providing general lounge facilities for approximately twenty persons. It must be equipped with settees, easy chairs, and tables. A pleasant and sunny prospect is essential, and the decoration and lighting must be quiet and restful as a relief from the glare of the stage lighting. The provision of a number of writing tables would be a welcome feature, and a small snack bar must be planned in conjunction with the room, where sandwiches and light drinks can be provided on 'heavy' days. Apart from its use during the performance of a play, the room will act as a club centre for the use of the company, giving them comforts and facilities not to be found in the average boarding house.

(*b*) DRESSING ROOMS

As has been suggested above, these can either be grouped around the stage block, or be arranged in a separate wing having access to the stage entry and assembly area on the prompt side of the stage.[1]

The average repertory theatre will need approximately twelve dressing rooms for the normal size company. These rooms may be planned for use as double rooms, with the exception of the three already mentioned, i.e. those of the producer, the stage director and the stage manager. In addition there should be two extra rooms capable of being used as chorus dressing rooms, each room accommodating up to ten persons; these would, however, be used only on special occasions, such as the visit of a ballet company, or for a heavy production.

Each of the double dressing rooms should be at least 10 ft.

[1] See *Home Office Manual*, 1934, section 19.

by 12 ft., and be planned as a shape approximating more to a square than to a long and narrow rectangle. The three office-dressing rooms should be planned to the same size, but each would be occupied by only one person. In each dressing room provision must be made for two separate dressing shelves or tables, rather than for one long shelf the length of the wall. Each table must be equipped with a mirror, and the room must be equipped with at least one full-length mirror. There should be hanging space for clothes, 2 ft. deep by 3 ft. wide, for each person, curtained off from the rest of the room, and, as the theatre may be used from time to time by outside companies, it would be as well to provide additional clothes space in the form of two locking wardrobes, each of which would allow an extra 3 ft. width of hanging space, with drawer space, and provision for shoes. In these wardrobes the resident company may lock away all their personal properties while having a week out. A wash-basin, with hot and cold running water, and a towel-rail must be provided in each room, and, in addition to the chairs for use at the dressing tables, two easy chairs should be provided for use when learning lines, or awaiting a call.

Every room must have natural lighting and ventilation in the form of a window, and if possible the rooms should be planned to allow for a good prospect from the windows, care being taken that these do not overlook a particularly noisy street or market place, otherwise the actor's concentration is liable to suffer. Although it must be possible to light the room by natural means, it is also imperative that making-up should be done solely by artificial light. It must therefore be possible to exclude daylight entirely from the room at will and for this purpose heavy curtains or blinds should be fitted to all the dressing room windows. Lights must be arranged around each mirror in addition to the general room lighting.

Linoleum is the best floor covering as this can be washed easily and cleaned if make-up is spilt on it, and, as members of the company may have to walk around in bare feet, small washable rugs should be provided. A further advantage, though not a necessity, would be the provision of a system of loudspeakers throughout the theatre, by means of which the actors could follow the course of the play.

The chorus dressing rooms, to take ten persons each, must have a clear floor space of at least 12 ft. by 20 ft. Two or three wash-basins will be needed and the room would best be planned to allow for two continuous dressing tables down the centre, the wall space being occupied by ranges of cupboards with sliding doors, in addition to curtained hanging space for the actors' clothes, so that the room may be used as additional wardrobe storage space when not in use as a dressing room. Again, it should be possible to black-out the room, and the provision of power points for use with electric irons would be an advantage, especially if the room is to provide occasional accommodation for the wardrobe department. There must be adequate equipment of mirrors as already stated in the case of the double dressing rooms.

(c) BATHS AND LAVATORIES

In conjunction with the dressing rooms, blocks of lavatories and baths must be planned so that these are available on every floor, and are directly accessible to each group of dressing rooms. If the dressing rooms are arranged on more than one floor it would be best to allow for males on one floor and females on the other. Two to three shower baths and one slipper bath must be provided for each sex. This latter provision is suggested here as few boarding houses seem to provide these elementary necessities, and, unless the scheme includes the provision of a hostel to be run in conjunction with the theatre, adequate provision must be made in the theatre building. Incidentally, the provision of a hostel in the town for the use of any member of the theatrical profession, whether permanent members of the repertory theatre or visiting companies to any of the theatres in the town, would fill a long felt need. The production of a south-sea drama calling for the use of plenty of wet-white in the make-up will quickly demonstrate the need for some sort of bath on the theatre premises.

(d) WARDROBE ROOMS AND DYE-SHOP

In addition to the store space available in the chorus rooms, a large room will be required with space for cutting, fitting, making and storing costumes. Facilities should be provided here for washing minor articles of clothing, and also for ironing costumes, curtains, chair covers and other materials. Allowance should be made for a cutting table 4 ft. 6 in. wide by from 6 to 9 ft. long, with access on all four sides, and there should be space for at least two sewing machines. These machines will be used not only for making costumes but also for curtains and even backcloths. Cupboard space for hanging curtains, costumes, wigs, etc., must be arranged all around the room, and a drying cupboard would be an added advantage. Although the theatre will probably start with a small stock of costumes and furnishings it is obviously to the advantage of the management to buy or make these items and add them to their own collection, where they can be reused or altered as the need arises, rather than to be continually laying out money on the hiring of such items with no long term advantage to themselves. The amount of space to be allocated to the wardrobe section is therefore a matter for the decision of the theatre promoters and will need to be proportionate to their policy on these matters. It may be decided that no special section should be allotted for this purpose, but in the long run this would be a short-sighted policy. A clear floor space, exclusive of cupboards, of 20 ft. by 12 ft. should serve the general purposes of this department well enough, with the provision of such additional storage space as the theatre promoters see fit.

Under this heading it will be necessary to discuss the provision of a dye-shop. If it is decided that costumes and furnishings are to be made in the theatre, then again it is an advantage if cheap materials can be dyed and printed to resemble more expensive fabrics, and the designer is able to have them produced to his own requirements rather than having to accept ready-made and possibly unsuitable materials. In this case a room for use as a dye-shop must be included, preferably close to the scene designer's quarters, where he can supervise the work. This room must accommodate a printing table 5 ft. wide by from 9 to 18 ft. long, in addition there will need to be drying racks, hung from the ceiling, on which lengths of material up to 54 in. wide may be hung in loops to dry after dying and printing. Space will also be required for a copper or boiler for 'fixing' purposes, a sink with hot and cold running water, a storage cupboard for dyes, and a small table for the preparation of printing screens.

(e) LIBRARY AND BOARD ROOM

This room may serve the double purpose and may well be placed at any convenient position in the building as may seem fit to the architect. The library would consist of a collection of play scripts and working copies, and would be available to the producer and stage director or to any member of the play-reading committee; it should not be made generally available to the theatre company. The room would be used mainly as a board room for the various theatre committees and should be planned as such, with any necessary provision for the housing of books as can be reasonably located around the walls. There should be, in addition, a small archives room for the storage of designs, models, theatre photographs, playbills, programmes, etc. If a drama school is to be planned as part of the theatre building, then a separate library, which would cater for the needs of the students and staff, must be included in addition to that already mentioned.

(f) STAGE DOORKEEPER'S ROOM

A small room will be required adjoining the main entrance to the back-stage portion of the building. It should be large enough to allow office accommodation for one man, who will control and supervise all entry into this portion of the building. Provision must be made here for letter racks and keyboard, and for a telephone for the use of the company, in addition to a house telephone communicating with the various offices in the theatre.

(g) BOX ROOM

A small room for the storage of theatrical hampers or trunks belonging to the members of the company must be provided. This room will most probably be under the control of the stage doorkeeper, and should, if possible, be planned adjacent to his room.

(h) STAFF GREEN-ROOM

Although not generally provided in existing theatre buildings this room is an absolute necessity. It must be placed conveniently near to, but out of earshot of, the stage—like the actors the stage staff too can be noisy when off-stage—and will be used mainly by the stage staff when waiting to be called for the next scene change. The room should therefore provide a degree of comfort, chairs and tables being provided, and also lockers where the staff may keep their overalls, and where they may lock up their outdoor clothing, shoes and boots, while wearing their theatre clothing. Unless some such provision is made it will be found almost impossible to insist on the stage crew changing into soft shoes or wearing gloves whilst shifting scenery; the former being necessary for quiet movement and the latter an essential feature when scenery painted in light tones is being handled. The room must be large enough to accommodate ten men comfortably.

(i) BILL STORE

If the theatre is to do its own bill-posting a small store will be needed for the use of the bill-poster. As it is more usual these days to contract this business to some outside firm, this room will probably be needed for the storage of such additional display work as may be limited to the theatre building itself. In this case the room would best be planned

H

in the front-of-house, and would be used for the storage of any removable lettering, picture frames, or other form of week to week advertising.

(*j*) STAFF LAVATORIES

Male staff lavatories must be planned near their staff room, and wash-basins must be included. These lavatories must be easily accessible both from the stage and from the workshop and painting area, care being taken to see that a male lavatory is available for the use of the flymen, whose post throughout the performance of the play will be on the working fly-gallery, usually that on the prompt side of the stage.

The cleaning of the stage and workshop areas is the duty of the stage staff and, since these staffs are usually male, no allowance for female staff lavatories need be made here, particularly since, as has already been suggested, lavatories for either sex should be planned directly adjoining the stage, and these may be available to all and sundry. The dressing-rooms, offices and corridors will be cleaned by the female staff of the theatre, who will be provided with a rest and changing room, and with lavatories, in the front-of-house section.

(*k*) BAND ROOM

For normal dramatic purposes the overture or interval music will probably be performed by a trio or quartet, a large orchestra being unnecessary except for ballet or other musical productions. The current practice of using recorded music in place of live musicians is to be deplored, as the presence of these performers helps to add to the intimate theatrical atmosphere which we are striving to achieve. It has been suggested that the musicians might use one of the stage boxes for the performance of their music, and this should be designed to accommodate three or four players who should be able to perform in full view of the audience.

The prompt side box being occupied by the electrician, the musicians must be accommodated in the O.P. box, and the band or rest room must be easily accessible both to this position and to the 'orchestra pit' should this ever be used. As a large orchestra would only occasionally be employed, it is hardly necessary to provide a large band room since normally accommodation would be required only for a maximum of three or four persons.

(*l*) PANATROPE ROOM

A small room large enough to accommodate a two-disc panatrope and no more than two persons. An average size of panatrope is 4 ft. by 2 ft. on plan. This room would best be planned in connection with the O.P. stage box where the musicians are accommodated, a space at the rear of the box being the most convenient position. There should be direct access by a small spiral stair to the assembly space under, and from there direct to the stage. Shelves for the storage of gramophone records must be built along the walls, and this space and the band space alongside must be connected to the stage director's control station by cue-light and telephone.

(*m*) QUICK-CHANGE ROOM

Two small rooms should be planned, one on either side of the stage, where an actor may make a quick-change. It may sometimes be necessary, in the course of a play, for an actor or actress to leave the acting area of the stage, make a complete change of clothes and reappear on the stage within a matter of seconds, and the quick-change room must therefore be as close and accessible to the acting area as it is possible to achieve. Each room must be large enough to accommodate one actor and a dresser, a full-length mirror must be included, and the room may be entirely lit by artificial light.

(*n*) REHEARSAL ROOMS

One rehearsal room at least must be provided for use when the stage is not available. The rehearsal room must be at least the size of the acting area of the stage, with a clear space of not less than 5 ft. all round. It should be possible to set out on the floor of this room the full shape of any set that is going to be used on the stage, so that the cast may rehearse under conditions similar to those in which they will be playing. It is important that the accoustics of the rehearsal room should, as nearly as possible, duplicate the conditions prevailing on the stage when it is in use. As few local authorities allow the use of the under-stage space as a scene store, and, since there is no stage machinery situated here, this area may be found to provide adequate space for a rehearsal room. If this area is to be used, it must have natural light and ventilation, and a direct exit to the open air will have to be provided.[2] An alternative arrangement is to build a separate rehearsal room or small hall, which can be let out as a dance hall or general lecture room when not in use by the company.

It has been mentioned earlier that the civic theatre might well form the central unit in a county drama scheme, and in this case provision must be made for an extra rehearsal room for the use of the touring company. As their plays will be performed in small village halls, the rehearsal room will not need to be large, and a space 24 ft. by 20 ft. should prove ample.

Mention has also been made of including a drama school in the theatre layout, and, if this factor is to be considered, then additional accommodation must be included: a number of lecture rooms must be provided which can also be used as rehearsal rooms, and a small experimental theatre to seat 200 to 300 persons would most probably be required. If such a theatre is to be included in the scheme it must be planned in such a position that its stage is readily available to the main workshop area of the civic theatre; it should then be possible to make use of this theatre as an additional rehearsal area.

(o) PASS DOORS

Although it has been the custom in the past to provide pass doors between the stage and the front-of-house through

_____
[2] See _Home Office Manual_, 1934, sections 16–18.

the auditorium, it is preferable to arrange that contact between these two sections should be possible without the necessity of passing through the auditorium. The two stage doors will provide the access from the stage to the auditorium necessary at rehearsals. The movement of theatre personnel through the theatre auditorium during a performance is most distracting to the audience, and any necessary passageways or service areas must be kept sufficiently remote from the auditorium, so that people in the audience are not disturbed by the sound of footsteps or chattering.

(p) BOILER AND PLENUM CHAMBERS

These must allow for the normal accommodation required in a building of the size under consideration here, and there are no special theatrical requirements. It should, however, be pointed out that there must be really adequate heating arrangements both in the dressing rooms and stage area, as actors and actresses may often have to perform plays in a certain degree of undress even in mid-winter, and, apart altogether from consideration for their comfort, bad conditions here make for poor work and large sickness incidence.[3]

[3] See: *Home Office Manual*, 1934, sections 80–85, 124–126.

Apart from the requirements of the auditorium proper, which have already been considered in a separate section, this area of the theatre will not be dealt with in great detail, as the accommodation required does not differ greatly from similar accommodation required in other buildings, and little special theatrical knowledge is required by the architect. There is, moreover, considerable data already available regarding the arrangements of cloakrooms, foyers, restaurants, etc., and in this section it will only be necessary to outline very briefly such items as need special attention in a building of this nature, and to give one or two general indications as to their disposal. When the design of this area is under consideration, lavish use should be made of colour to achieve an air of gaiety and pleasure, not only in the decoration of the building itself, but in the use of flowering shrubs and trees, flower-beds and boxes, colourful paintings and murals and the use of sculpture. Cleanliness, efficiency and enjoyment are the key notes in the design and running of a good civic theatre.

(*a*) BOX OFFICE

This room must be available at the main entrance foyer of the building, but it must also connect with a small hallway or covered area set outside the main buildings, which can be used during the daytime, or at such times as the main theatre building is closed, as an advance booking office. The room must allow space for two clerks, be at least 8 ft. by 12 ft., and must have some form of natural ventilation, as it will be in continuous use throughout the day and evening.

(*b*) MANAGER'S OFFICE

Arranged with the box office there must be a suite of offices for the general manager of the theatre and his staff.

The general manager will be responsible for running the business side of the theatre and the company, as distinct from the artistic side. His duties involve the payment of all persons employed in the building, and he is in charge of all theatre finances; he is also responsible for all publicity work and public relations. He will require an office in which to carry on his work, and a room, or rooms, will be required for the use of the assistant manager and at least one secretary. Lavatory and washing facilities must be available in this suite, and it should be remembered that the manager will have to change into evening dress before attending in the foyer each evening to welcome the audience.

(c) FOYERS AND CLOAKROOMS

The main entrance foyer must be planned on an open and generous scale, and the public must have direct access to the cloakrooms and lavatories. It is of the utmost importance that an easy flow of visitors should be maintained both entering and leaving the theatre building, and the cloakroom accommodation must be planned to deal with the maximum number of persons in the minimum time. This point is particularly neglected in some of the older theatres, and architects may well give it special consideration. It is better to provide a large area of counter space in the cloakrooms and to put extra staff on duty during rush hours, than to attempt to deal with the sudden rushes of visitors inevitable in theatre business with minimum staff and counter space. Speed, efficiency and courtesy are the prime considerations to be borne in mind when planning this area of the building. Bad front-of-house management and conditions can wreck the chances of any theatre company however good their productions may be, and this is particularly true when it is desired to build up and maintain a regular audience in a small town.

Wide, easy-going staircases must connect the entrance foyer with the lounge space over, and with the various areas of the auditorium. Every opportunity must be taken to build up a dramatic approach, both to the theatre building itself, and, once inside the building, to the auditorium and the play; an approach which has the special quality implicit in the very idea of theatre and the drama.

(d) LOUNGE SPACE

As the auditorium will be planned in, at most, two main sections, it would be as well to connect both sections with one lounge. This should be planned as a fine open area, with views through large windows over the civic centre or park and gardens. Space must be planned here for exhibitions of theatre paintings, models, etc., and there must be comfortable seating arrangements for members of the audience making this their meeting place before having a meal, and spending the evening at the play. This area may well connect with an open terrace or balcony for use in the summer, and direct connection should be arranged with the restaurant and tea-room.

Many civic theatres have found it advisable to run a club, or community centre, in connection with their theatre, thereby allowing for a greater social intimacy between the players and their public, and at the same time building up a subscription audience. In this case the provision of various club-rooms would be a necessary additional feature, and these, in connection with the lounge and exhibition areas, would be used for various club functions such as dinners, lectures, informal talks or dances.

(e) BARS

Directly connected with the lounge there should be a bar, but this must be so designed as to allow for its being closed to the public out of licensing hours; on the other hand it must be capable of dealing with the rush which always takes place during each interval. This area, and indeed any area where noisy use is likely to be made of glass or crockery, or where the customers or staff are likely to carry on conversations during the performance of a play, should be planned to eliminate all possibility of the sounds penetrating to the auditorium.

(f) RESTAURANT AND TEA-ROOM

The restaurant and tea-room may be planned as one unit, on one or two floors, and may be served by the same kitchen; both should be accessible to the theatre lounge, but they should be open to the general public as well as to the theatre-goer, and must therefore be planned to allow for easy control of persons who may wish to enter the theatre from either section.

In addition there should be an open-air tea-terrace for use when summer weather permits. Plentiful use should be made here of flower-beds and boxes, and shade may be provided by the planting of small flowering trees, and by the use of colourful awnings and sun-shades.

Space for the accommodation of a small band, or of the theatre musicians, should be planned both on the terrace and in the restaurant and tea-room.

The kitchens, stores and other rooms necessary for this group should be planned in accordance with any local regulations, and should be so placed that their service yards and entrances do not interfere with the public enjoyment of the theatre building. Office and lavatory accommodation for the restaurant manager must be provided, and if non-theatre-going public are to be admitted to the restaurant, lavatory accommodation must be included for them.

(g) STAFF ROOM

A general staff room and changing room for the use of the female staff of the building may be designed in connection with this section, and provision should be made here for the general cleaners, programme sellers and other female staff, in addition to the staff employed in the restaurant and tea-room. Lavatory accommodation must be arranged in connection with this room. If male staff are to be employed in the restaurant a separate changing room and lavatory must be provided for them.

15. *Summary*

IN OUR GENERATION the theatre occupies a high place in
public esteem. In a clearer historical perspective our view
of its social significance is developing rapidly, and this is
leading to a demand for its work which is vocal amongst the
most responsible leaders of public opinion.

The aim of the author of this book has been to smooth
the path for those civic authorities and their architects who
approach the task, undoubtedly novel in municipal enterprise, of planning a theatre that shall be worthy of their city
and at the same time be pre-eminently a workmanlike piece
of civic building.

The plans that are suggested here may appear lavish against
the sombre background of this decade's stringencies, but
they represent little more than minimum requirements for
adequate building, and are in fact considerably less lavish
than many such theatre buildings on the continent of Europe:
funds for these theatres were in many cases raised wholly by
public subscription, here we have the additional benefit of
official expenditure from the rates, which may be set aside
against the time when general building operations are again
possible.

It will not elude the imagination of officials charged with
the responsibility for developing municipal enterprise, that
the odd ha'p'orth of tar required to perfect this ship is well
worth the outlay; once launched, it will bring rich argosies
down the years in the form of buoyant business built by the
curiosity and interest of visitors from all over the country,
and indeed from all over the world, who come to see British
drama played in an ideal setting.

The revenue earning ability of theatre enterprise depends
unquestionably upon the quality of the enterprise: the half-
baked scheme were better never begun. This particular

enterprise must be given every assistance in the form of a perfect theatre, and it must be remembered that it will have to compete with many other forms of entertainment; unless the potential audience can be offered amenities comparable with those offered by the other forms, the theatre company will find themselves working against impossible odds.

We cannot do better, as we take leave of our readers, than to speed with good wishes every enterprise that sets as its aim the designing of a theatre worthy of the high tradition of our dramatic literature, worthy too to play host from time to time to the greatest dramatic companies and literary achievements from all over the world.

This book is set in Monotype Caslon Old Face, a design based on the matrices cut by William Caslon I in 1772. Caslon, in turn, used as his model some Dutch faces which enjoyed great popularity at the time, particularly the type designed by Christopher Van Dyck.

Caslon Old Face was the work of a craftsman who had to cut all his punches by hand and was therefore free to vary the individual letter in weight and shape from size to size. The italic series has several decorated capitals known as swash characters which give particular grace and beauty to the face.